Rooted Again

Re-Establishing Forgotten or
Abandoned Connections with God
and God's Kingdom Mandate

LILLIAN C. SMITH

WESTBOW
PRESS®
A DIVISION OF THOMAS NELSON
& ZONDERVAN

This book is a work of non-fiction. Unless otherwise noted, the author and the publisher
make no explicit guarantees as to the accuracy of the information contained in this book
and in some cases, names of people and places have been altered to protect their privacy.

WestBow Press books may be ordered through booksellers or by contacting:

WestBow Press
A Division of Thomas Nelson & Zondervan
1663 Liberty Drive
Bloomington, IN 47403
www.westbowpress.com
844-714-3454

Because of the dynamic nature of the Internet, any web addresses or links contained in
this book may have changed since publication and may no longer be valid. The views
expressed in this work are solely those of the author and do not necessarily reflect the
views of the publisher, and the publisher hereby disclaims any responsibility for them.

Any people depicted in stock imagery provided by Getty Images are models,
and such images are being used for illustrative purposes only.
Certain stock imagery © Getty Images.

Scripture quotations marked (NIV) are taken from the Holy Bible, New
International Version®, NIV®. Copyright © 1973, 1978, 1984, 2011 by Biblica,
Inc.® Used by permission of Zondervan. All rights reserved worldwide. www.
zondervan.com The "NIV" and "New International Version" are trademarks
registered in the United States Patent and Trademark Office by Biblica, Inc.®

Scripture marked (KJV) taken from the King James Version of the Bible.

ISBN: 978-1-6642-8231-5 (sc)
ISBN: 978-1-6642-8230-8 (e)

Print information available on the last page.

WestBow Press rev. date: 11/09/2022

CONTENTS

ACKNOWLEDGEMENTS

The All Wise, All-Knowing God is the reason I had the opportunity to pursue a Doctor of Ministry degree and complete research project which forms the basis of this book. I will be forever thankful for You ordering my steps to this time and place. For your abundant provision, guidance, and love, I thank you. God, your favor is amazing, and your promises are true. May this project give you glory and strengthen congregations to fulfill their mission of making disciples of Jesus Christ who will transform the world with love, on your behalf.

With loving gratitude, Lillian

DEDICATION

To my family who journeyed with me on this adventure-my husband David Cassidy, Magnificent Mom-Doris Hall and my two sons Charles Jasper "CJ" and Hayward Smith-Cassidy. To my father, the late Rev. C. Jasper Smith, you are gone but not forgotten.

To the Cheverly United Methodist Church family for their heart for God, Cheverly, 20785 and beyond. To those who, sacrificed their time, prayed and worked to help CUMC be a part of what God is doing in their community in this new season – Janet Adams, Donna and Dwight Brown, Carolyn Nash Burgess, Brian Frye, James Jenkins, Teaira Parker, Denise Robinson, Hayward Smith-Cassidy, Elizabeth "Lizz" and Maurice Stewart, Chrishan Thuraisingham, and Karen White,

To the exegetical reflection group – Karen White and Larry and Joyce Woodworth. To my professional and contextual mentors- Bishop Marcus Matthew, the Rev. Dr. Yvonne Wallace Penn, the Rev. Dr. James Shopshire, the Rev. Dr. E. Allen Stewart and Dr. June Fair.

To My Peers in the first Rooted Section – the Rev. Zach Beasley and the Rev. Rudy Rasmus. We are in it together.

To My Doctor of Ministry Cohort – Rooted: Church Planting and Church Revitalization in Our Diverse World and our mentors, the Rev. Dr. Rosario Picardo and the Rev. Dr. Vance P. Ross and Faculty Advisor, the Rev. Dr. Joni Sancken

To God- Father, Son and Holy Spirit – For Your Glory

The Rev. Dr. Lillian Catherine Smith Cassidy has a heart of a pastor. She has communicated a vision that includes action steps required to turn visions into realities for Cheverly UMC. Lillian demonstrates that mission and discipleship making are inextricably linked. As Cheverly UMC or any local church seeks to engage the world in mission on behalf of the living Christ, the membership will become more intimately involved in the process of discipleship making.

Bishop Marcus Matthews, Retired, The United Methodist Church

"Your success as a disciple of Christ is not something you do; it is someone you disciple to also become a disciple-maker."

_Jonathan Hayashi, *Ordinary Radicals: A Return to Christ-Centered Discipleship*

ONE

Ministry Focus

The Vine - Plant Connection

SOME OF THE MOST BEAUTIFUL plants are vines. Boston ivy, Chilean jasmine (Mandevilla laxa), Star jasmine and honeysuckle are just a few flowering vines. Grapes, cucumbers, and tomatoes are fruit that grow on vines. The fruit or flower grows in connection to the vine. Apart from the vine, no fruit or flower grows. The vitality and vibrancy of the fruit or flower is determined by the nutrition it gets from the vine.

The health and vitality of a congregation is similar to that of a fruit or flower. Apart from an intimate and abiding relationship with Jesus Christ, Christians, and Christian congregations wither on the vine. It is only Jesus' delegated authority, power, and anointing that enable us to minister on his behalf. What we do on our own human strength produces weak results. Externally, circumstances may appear fine; yet, without the connection or anointing from God, death is certain, no matter how long the process takes.

This book grew out of my Doctor of Ministry studies at United Theological Seminary, where I participated in the cohort, "Rooted: Church Planting and Church Revitalization in Our Diverse World." My time in the cohort reinforced pastoral experience and observations. The context of my Doctor of Ministry research project was Cheverly United Methodist Church, where I serve as pastor. The congregation I serve mirrors the ministry reality of many mainline churches. Most, if not all churches started out on fire for God and on mission to lift up Jesus and 'rescue the perishing.' Yet, through the passing of years, shifts took place which resulted in a disconnect from God and God's kingdom mandate.

Congregations that are disconnected from the God who called them, lose focus of, and often forget their kingdom assignment. Disconnected from the true vine, Jesus, we lack power. Life-transforming ministry is not based on committee membership or being on the church's rolls. Rather, it is reflective of an abiding relationship with Jesus Christ, empowered by the Holy Spirit and lived out through a life of discipleship.

> [5] I am the vine; you are the branches. If you remain in me and I in you, you will bear much fruit; apart from me you can do nothing. [6] If you do not remain in me, you are like a branch that is thrown away and withers; such branches are picked up, thrown into the fire and burned. [7] If you remain in me and my words remain in you, ask whatever you wish, and it will be done for you. [8] This is to my Father's glory, that you bear much fruit, showing yourselves to be my disciples.
> [1] John 15: 5-8 NIV

It is easy to become busy doing the work of religion and dismiss the importance of a personal and growing relationship with the living Christ. Our relationship with Jesus Christ directs our personal faith walk. It is easy to allow our spiritual connection to God to diminish. John Wesley voiced the concern about that possibility in the 18th century. In "Thoughts Upon Methodism," Wesley wrote,

> I am not afraid that the people called Methodists should ever cease to exist either in Europe or America. But I am afraid that lest they should only exist as a dead sect, having the form of religion without the power. And this undoubtedly will be the case unless they hold fast both the doctrine, spirit, and discipline with which they first set out.[2]

Most United Methodist believers can quote the mission of the church: "to make disciples of Jesus Christ for the Transformation of the World."[3]

---

[1] Biblegateway, accessed on December 17, 2017, https://www.biblegateway.com/passage/?search=John+15, NIV.

[2] John Wesley, "Thoughts Upon Methodism," London, August 4, 1786, accessed on December 12, 2016, file:///C:/Users/pastor/Downloads/THOUGHTS_UPON_METHODISM.PDF.

[3] United Methodist Mission Statement, accessed on December 28, 2017, http://www.umc.org/news-and-media/united-methodist-mission-statement-revised.

However, many may not know that the mission includes sharing your faith with others and inviting them to know, love, and follow Jesus. Some may not know that to live out that mission has the desired outcome of new disciples. To make a disciple requires one to live as a disciple. To live as a disciple necessitates knowing and understanding the benefits, roles, and responsibilities of a disciple. Discipleship entails a lifestyle of intentional growth and service.

Jesus explained the importance of staying connected to him.

> I am the true vine, and my Father is the husbandman. ² Every branch in me that beareth not fruit he taketh away: and every branch that beareth fruit, he purgeth it, that it may bring forth more fruit. ³ Now ye are clean through the word which I have spoken unto you. ⁴ Abide in me, and I in you. As the branch cannot bear fruit of itself, except it abide in the vine; no more can ye, except ye abide in me.[4]
> John 15: 1-5, KJV

Fruit develops from the nourishment that comes from the vine. The fruit we bear is evidenced by our ability to touch people's lives in ways that give them opportunities to know, love, and follow Jesus. Fruit can be seen when hurting and broken communities are changed by the power of God's loving grace. Fruit can be seen in how we live our lives. People will know we are Christians through our ability to love one another. Evidence of our connection to Christ is seen as we help hurting people encounter a loving God, who offers abundance and spiritual freedom. On our own strength, we can do nothing.

> ⁵ I am the vine, ye are the branches: He that abideth in me, and I in him, the same bringeth forth much fruit: for without me ye can do nothing. ⁶ If a man abide not in me, he is cast forth as a branch, and is withered; and men gather them, and cast them into the fire, and they are burned. ⁷ If ye abide in me, and my words abide in you, ye shall ask what ye will, and it shall be done unto you. ⁸ Herein is my Father glorified, that ye bear much fruit; so shall ye be my disciples.[5]

---

[4]   John 15: 1-4, Bible gateway, accessed August 19, 2022 https://www.biblegateway.com/passage/?search=John%2015%3A1-5&version=KJV

[5]   John 15: 5-8, BibleGateway, accessed on August 19, 2022, https://www.biblegateway.com/passage/?search=John+15%3A+5-8&version=KJV.

Lillian C. Smith

Strengthening the Vine Connection in the Church

Reflecting on the imagery of the vine, a few questions present themselves to congregations today. If a congregation is growing in its discipleship, will it live out an understanding of mission and ministry that intentionally strives to bring people into relationship with Jesus Christ? Does our growth as Christ followers in the areas of Bible study, worship and other spiritual disciplines affect the level or effectiveness of ministry? Will strengthening our vine connection with Jesus Christ enhance our ministry and cause us to be more externally focused? How does our connection to Christ influence our ministry? Does a growing discipleship result in congregational outreach in their neighborhood? How can we encourage others to become better connected to the Vine—the Christ? Can an established congregation regain a desire to build bridges to the community that surrounds them? What role does discipleship play in the mission, outreach, and evangelism of a congregation? This book will highlight the importance of congregants shifting from the mindset of member to that of a disciple. There is a difference.

It is my belief that disciple making in many congregations has diminished, which was both caused by and has resulted in a loss of understanding of the mission of the church and a low prioritization of reaching new people for Christ. In many instances, the new people are outside the church walls in our neighborhoods. In other situations, people come into our church buildings to meet, but not to engage in the ministry of the church. It is vitally important to create pathways for discipleship to encourage and empower spiritual growth for Christ followers. In stronger connection with the vine, Jesus Christ, we will have the strength, power, and anointing to effectively minister. The project will also create a bridge by which congregations and community members can develop relationships and ministry to the community. It is my contention that people who are intentionally growing in their discipleship will bridge the divides that separate us to share their faith and invite their friends, relatives, associates, and neighbors to church or church offerings—studies, mission outreach, etc. The result of spiritual growth, coupled with intentional bridge building, can and should result in growth.

TWO

Biblical Foundations

Spiritual Memory Loss Has Hampered Discipleship

WHAT IS THE CHURCH AND what is its purpose? Is it for Christians to gather each week for worship? As many US congregations address the growing number of "nones," individuals with no religious affiliation, and declining worship attendance, these and other questions are being discussed in earnest.

According to the 2014 Pew Religious Landscape Study, 23% of the US population are classified as religious "nones." Nones, many of whom were previously churched, "self-identify as atheists or agnostics, ...or nothing in particular." [6] A major cause of concern is the growing number of young people who are "nones." In 2014, research revealed the following:

> Overall, religiously unaffiliated people are more concentrated among young adults than other age groups – 35% of Millennials (those born 1981-1996) are "nones." In addition, the unaffiliated as a whole are getting even younger. The median age of unaffiliated adults is now 36, down from 38 in 2007 and significantly younger than the overall median age of U.S. adults in 2014 (46).[7]

---

[6] Michael Lipka,"A closer look at America's rapidly growing religious nones." Pew Research Center, accessed March 31, 2017, http://www.pewresearch.org/fact-tank/2015/05/13/a-closer-look-at-americas-rapidly-growing-religious-nones/.

[7] Lipka, "A closer look at America's rapidly growing religious nones."

The church is more than a place where the neighborhood gathers. Congregations are more than communities of believers that provide social services to hurting people. The church of Jesus Christ is a community of believers that has the mission of fulfilling the Great Commission undergirded by the Great Commandment. Churches have the mission of "making disciples of Jesus Christ" and loving their neighbors as themselves. In the words of Marlon Hall, Curator, Awakenings Movement, churches are "Incubators of Disruptive Innovators of Faith" who have the mission and assignment of helping to bring God's kingdom in their families, homes, communities and nations." [8] Christians are called to make a difference.

Christian believers represent the diversity of all that which is human. The diversity spans colors, languages, cultures, ethnicities, genders, generations, and socio-economic realities. Ideally, the mixed multitude of believers meet for worship, study, fellowship and to be equipped to live as disciples. Issues of race, culture, socio-economic and other concerns have caused people not to be welcome in numerous congregations. Worship segregated by color, race, and ethnicity still is a persistent reality in the US. In many regards, the church is perceived as irrelevant or out of touch with the world.

What happens when Christ followers, or disciples, forget their purpose for being? The ultimate mission of the church is to make disciples of Jesus Christ. Disciples are charged to make disciples. Although the mission is established, disciple-making in many congregations is all but an endangered endeavor. It is my contention that this reality may exist due to misplaced prioritization that more highly values:

- Hospitality, in the form of building usage extended toward community members and organizations instead of evangelism/faith sharing
- Attending to the work of the church rather than attending to ministry unto the Lord
- Maintaining and addressing the needs of those already in congregations versus inviting non-church members to join them in their faith journey with Christ
- Maintenance of the status quo instead of "social disruption"

---

[8] Marlon Hall, from his presentation, "Film and Innovation," delivered at the Immerse Conference: Where Spirituality and Innovation Connect. St. John's Downtown, Houston, TX, March 17, 2017.

- An inwardly focused perspective instead of an externally focused ministry and outreach approach
- Homogeneous ministry versus multi-ethnic, multi-cultural and diverse ministry
- Discipleship in many established congregations is a challenged reality
- Evangelism is avoided because many believe all religions are equal and Jesus is not really needed because all paths lead to God.
- The notion of evangelism is offensive to many within the church.

Research indicates that most Christians do not participate in on-going Christian discipleship.

> "…only 20 percent of Christian adults are involved in some sort of discipleship activity—and this includes a wide range of activities such as attending Sunday school or fellowship group, meeting with a spiritual mentor, studying the Bible with a group, or reading and discussing a Christian book with a group. [9]

Congregations exist to love and serve God. That love and service to God, lived out through methods or ministries, does not always result in new disciples. For example, a congregation's feeding ministry to needy neighbors does not necessarily include an intention to share Jesus, who is the ultimate bread of life, as well as earthly food.

Congregations with the spiritual gift of hospitality may provide space for many community organizations to meet in the building but might never offer those guests in the building an opportunity to enter into the life of the church or into a personal relationship with Jesus Christ along. Spiritual hospitality is invaluable. It alone is not enough. Conversely, numerous congregations are friendly towards those individuals who are a part of their worshiping community but are not welcoming towards others who come from distinctly different or diverse backgrounds – gender, generation, ethnic/cultural, orientation, etc. A congregation's heart for the

---

[9]   David Kinnamon, "New Research on the State of Discipleship," Research Releases in Leaders & Pastors, December 1, 2015, accessed on April 2, 2017, https://www.barna.com/research/new-research-on-the-state-of-discipleship/.

community does not inherently demonstrate a love that invites people to come into a reconciled, transformed relationship with Jesus Christ.

Congregations would benefit from the creation of intentional disciple-making opportunities for those whom God brings into their church buildings, neighbors, as well as those who are already a part of the worshipping community. Disciples make disciples. Strengthening the church's disciple-making system will strengthen the congregation's kingdom building efforts. A strong disciple making system will help the congregation identify and seize opportunities to create connections with community members and facilitate the development of relationships and ministry to and with the community.

The harvest is literally outside the walls of our churches. In some instances, God is bringing the harvest into our buildings. Often, community organizations meet in our churches. It is my hope and prayer that this book will encourage and empower spiritual growth for Christ followers and congregations. Prayerfully, this book will spark opportunities for those who are already present in the community of faith to grow in their discipleship so that they can help neighbors, friends, relatives, and associates grow in their faith. We can't make disciples if we are not disciples.

In stronger connection with Jesus Christ, the vine, we will have the strength, power and anointing to effectively minister, as strong branches, to bear fruit as evidenced by new people engaging in ministry and conversions. People who are intentionally growing in their discipleship will be more open to bridge the divides that separate those in and outside of the church.

Revisiting the Kingdom Mandate in Scripture

In this book, we will engage and address two scriptures - Isaiah 56: 1-8 and Acts 10: 44-48. Both scriptures communicate God's radical love for all people – those who are born with a relationship with God and those, on the periphery who may want that relationship but not know how to get there; individuals who have not been invited or may feel condemned and unworthy to be a part of the Christian community. We can't forget those who don't want any religious affiliation. Both passages address people born into the household of faith and those who are not.

We will first engage Isaiah 56: 1-8 and discuss the three elements of dating, content, and structure. This component will also highlight language or literary concerns. This chapter will also discuss the three elements of dating, content and structure and literary concerns for Acts 10: 44-48. Finally, this book will demonstrate how these scriptural passages are relevant to our current reality.

OLD TESTAMENT/HEBREW BIBLE PASSAGE

ISAIAH 56: 1-8

Isaiah 56:1-8 New International Version (NIV)

Salvation for Others

This is what the Lord says:
"Maintain justice
and do what is right,
for my salvation is close at hand
and my righteousness will soon be revealed.
2 Blessed is the one who does this—
the person who holds it fast,
who keeps the Sabbath without desecrating it,
and keeps their hands from doing any evil."
3 Let no foreigner who is bound to the Lord say,
"The Lord will surely exclude me from his people."
And let no eunuch complain,
"I am only a dry tree."
4 For this is what the Lord says:
"To the eunuchs who keep my Sabbaths,
who choose what pleases me
and hold fast to my covenant—
5 to them I will give within my temple and its walls
a memorial and a name
better than sons and daughters;
I will give them an everlasting name

that will endure forever.
⁶ And foreigners who bind themselves to the Lord
to minister to him,
to love the name of the Lord,
and to be his servants,
all who keep the Sabbath without desecrating it
and who hold fast to my covenant—
⁷ these I will bring to my holy mountain
and give them joy in my house of prayer.
Their burnt offerings and sacrifices
will be accepted on my altar;
for my house will be called
a house of prayer for all nations."
⁸ The Sovereign Lord declares—
he who gathers the exiles of Israel:
"I will gather still others to them
besides those already gathered."[10]

This passage concentrates on the promise of salvation for those who previously were excluded from the community of believers and responsibilities in the sanctuary. What would have caused a change in message about inclusion and exclusion? Did God's purpose or ultimate plan change? What other issues existed?

In this endeavor of biblical inquiry and exegetical work, it was interesting to obtain insights about this passage from members of the congregation I serve. Three others joined me in the engagement of this text. Larry and Joyce W., an Anglo-American retired married couple who grew up in this church. Karen, an Anglo-American female church member also participated in this journey with me. Larry and Joyce shared the following about their encounter with this passage.

> Our understanding is that this scripture is part of "3ʳᵈ Isaiah" probably during the period after the return from exile when the returnees were faced with new issues: their relationship with the indigenous people and more broadly with questions

---

[10] Isaiah 56: 1-8, New International Version, accessed on December 5, 2017, https://www.biblegateway.com/passage/?search=Isaiah%2056:1-8.

of inclusivity and exclusivity. The writer here is arguing for inclusivity. Thus, foreigners and eunuchs who join themselves to God's people are to be welcomed and accepted as long as they are willing to keep the covenant commandments, especially keeping the Sabbath and refraining from doing evil. The passage builds to verse 7 which states that "my house shall be called a house of prayer for all peoples." Taken at face value that means that the Jewish people will welcome those who wish to join them, even those like foreigners or eunuchs who might be considered ritually unclean.

Isaiah 56 marks the transition from exile to postexilic existence. The community, to which this passage was addressed, was comprised of people who had returned from Babylonian exile. The transition from exile also qualifies the shift from the Deutero-Isaiah, DI, redactor to the Trito-Isaiah, TI, redactor.

The prophetic book of Isaiah reflects the work of at least three authors, whose work spans centuries. The original writer, for whom the book is named, is attributed authorship for most of the chapters of 1-39. The prophet Isaiah ministered from around 742 BCE until either 701 or 687 BCE. Beginning his ministry when King Uzziah died, he served during the reigns of Ahaz and Hezekiah. Spanning chapters 40-55, the writing of Second Isaiah, is attributed to either one author or a school of writers who were part of an "Isaiah school" of disciples. Second Isaiah is thought to have been written during the sixth century BCE. Third Isaiah comprises chapters 56-66 and is thought to have been written during the fifth century BCE. [11] The categorization of First, Second and Third Isaiah is influenced by elements and references of the biblical passages, such as historical information or references that are dated using extracanonical sources.

Back to the Trito-Isaiah, or TI. In Isaiah 56: 1-8, God reframes "who belongs" in the community of believers, (Isaiah 56: 3,4,5,6,7). This reframing may have addressed conflict within the community about who was rightfully a member. The post exilic faith community appears to have been experiencing challenges related to inclusivity and exclusivity.

---

[11]   Peter Enns, "Isaiah" Copyright 2011-2017, accessed on March 31, 2017, http://thecenterforbiblicalstudies.org/resources/introductions-to-the-books-of-the-bible/isaiah/; Paul Achtemeier, *Harper's Bible Dictionary*, (San Francisco, CA: Harper Collins, 1985), 426-431.

Who had the right to be in the community of faith? Now back in their homeland, others, or newcomers, are now adhering to the faith in their Adonai Elohim. Are these newcomers to enjoy covenant relationship and privileges? Most critical in this passage is God's reminder of the tenets of justice, righteousness and salvation to this community seeking to return to Israel and Judea. The next passage, Isaiah 56: 9-57:13, issues a strong rebuke of sorts for priests.

Related to foreigners, the issue of concern may not have centered on everyone, yet individuals who had previously chosen not to be a part of the community of believers. Resident aliens had long been a part of the worshipping community. This passage focuses on those who had not made the full commitment to God. The difference in terms used to refer to foreigners was ger and ben-nekar. The term ger refers to (resident aliens, sojourners) and ben-nekar (general foreigners or outsiders).[12] The term used in this passage is ben-nekar. John Goldingay suggests and explains that this scriptural passage not only addressed the inclusion of non-Jewish people into the community of faith but Jewish adherence to God's covenant ways.

> It will emerge that Isaiah 56-66 is concerned that many members of the Judahite community do not properly observe the Sabbath, and that this is not the only problem about their commitment to Yhwh's covenant. Yet it not implausible to imagine these people being strict about the exclusion of eunuchs and foreigners from worship of YHWH; they could easily make a case from the Torah for such a stance. The present passage thus turns their stance on its head. [13]

Two major themes, found in Isaiah 56:1, are justice and righteous. Both concepts are born out of the covenantal relationship with God and the communal relationships with others. Interestingly, the terms

---

[12] John Goldingay, "Isaiah 56: 1-8" *Isaiah 56-66 (ICC): A Critical and Exegetical Commentary*. London: Bloomsbury Publishing, 2014, 72, accessed on February 5, 2018, http://dx.doi.org/10.5040/9781472556158.0008; Yochanan Zaqantov, "The Ger, Gur, Zur, Nekar, Nakar, Goy and Lavah,"accessed on February 12, 2018, http://www.karaitejudaism.org/talks/Ger_Naker_Goy.pdf.

[13] John Goldingay, "Isaiah 56: 1-8" *Isaiah 56-66 (ICC): A Critical and Exegetical Commentary*. London, England: Bloomsbury Publishing, 2014, 75, accessed on February 5, 2018, http://dx.doi.org/10.5040/9781472556158.0008.

righteousness and justice share the same Hebrew term, צְדָקָה.[14] A noun, it is the feminine form of the word, transliterated as tsedaqah. Justice is reflective of the very nature of God. The Merriam Webster Dictionary provides the following as a definition of justice, "the quality of being just, impartial, or fair." [15] The concept of righteousness is contrary to a Western worldview which views the word as legalistic. "Righteousness as it is understood in the OT is a thoroughly Hebraic concept, foreign in the Western mind and at variance with the common understanding of the term."[16] Righteousness is based out of relationships – between humanity and God as well as between one another in community. With a Hebraic understanding, "...righteousness is in the OT the fulfillment of the demands of a relationship, whether that relationship be with men or with God."[17] Central to God's message in Isaiah 56: 1-8, is a divine reminder that God's people are called to be in right relationship with God and each other. That reality is not just confined to those who are born into the Jewish community, but those who have been grafted in.

There appear to have been issues in the community which required a response by way of changed behavior. To not continue in a life of justice and righteousness would have implications related to God's divine judgement. The redactor reminds the community that continuing as the beloved community is important because both God's judgement and salvation are forthcoming. No matter how long it takes, salvation and judgement would come. This passage is identified by some, not as instruction, but strong encouragement to live accordingly.

Salvation, vs. 1, is a phrase which encompasses a wide spectrum of understanding which includes "deeds of deliverance, help, prosperity, save, saving, and victories.[18] "יְשׁוּעָה, **yeshuah,** the Hebrew term, is a feminine

---

14 "Strong's Concordance "6666, Tsedaqah," accessed on March 23, 2017, http://biblehub.com/hebrew/6666.htm.

15 Merriam-Webster Dictionary, accessed on March 23, 2017, https://www.merriam-webster.com/dictionary/justice/.

16 *The Interpreter's Dictionary of the Bible: An Illustrated Encyclopedia, R-Z, Volume 4.* (Nashville, TN: Abingdon Press,1962, 17th Printing 1989), 80.

17 *The Interpreter's Dictionary of the Bible: An Illustrated Encyclopedia, R-Z, Volume 4, 80.*

18 Strong's Concordance, "3444. Yeshuah: salvation," accessed on March 23, 2017, http://biblehub.com/hebrew/3444.htm.

noun."[19] Jesus' very name means Jehovah is Salvation or Yahweh saves. God's saving and deliverance, or salvation, is not just limited to Israel, but everyone. Those formerly excluded who, in loving devotion to God, observe the Sabbath and God's covenant, will receive divine blessing.

God includes immigrants and eunuchs as part of his community of blessing, as they are now included in the list with the faithful. Jewish believers are instructed to welcome them. This new instruction is a stark revision of previous divine instruction. Previously, immigrants and eunuchs were forbidden from being in the sanctuary. (Leviticus 22: 24-25 & Ezekiel 44: 7-9). They were also forbidden from serving as priests in the temple. The redactor of Isaiah 56: 1-8 seems to turn the previous teachings upside down.

The biblical author appears to fulfill the purpose of helping formerly exiled individuals redefine what God desires for this community of Israelites. Exile changes the religious and social perspectives of a community. Israelite believers came under the influence of the cultural and religious mores of a foreign land. Jacob L. Wright and Michael J. Chan cited the work of other commentators who identify this pericope as a "prophetic Torah,"[20] as it appears to change the law laid out in the Pentateuch. The change may indicate that people, born outside of the Israelite community, now joined formerly exiled Israelites who returned to their homeland. Just as the previously exiled Israelites were influenced by other religions and practices while in a strange land, they also would have influenced others.

Whether or not this passage directly addresses the presence of eunuchs and immigrant males as priests is not clear in this text. What is clear is that previously, they were forbidden from serving in the temple. In Ezekiel 44, God rebukes the priests because they allowed foreigners to be in the sanctuary, serving as priests. "Thus saith the Lord GOD; No

---

[19] Strong's Concordance, "3444. Yeshuah: salvation," accessed on March 23, 2017.

[20] Raymond de Hoop, "The Interpretation of Isaiah 56: 1-9, Comfort or Criticism?" *Journal of Biblical Literature,* 127, no 4, (2008): 671; Jacob L. Wright and Michael J. Chan, "King and Eunuch: Isaiah 56:1- 8 in Light of Honorific Royal Burial Practices," *Journal of Biblical Literature* 131, no. 1 (2012):100, accessed on March 21, 2017, http://web.a.ebscohost.com.utsdayton.idm.oclc.org/ehost/detail/detail?vid=7&sid=566d7b02-cb1f-4f22-845a-39589eaeeb6e%40session mgr4007&bdata=JnNpdGU9ZWhvc3QtbGl2ZQ%3d%3d#db=rfh&AN=A TLA0001886158.

stranger, uncircumcised in heart, nor uncircumcised in flesh, shall enter into my sanctuary, of any stranger that is among the children of Israel.""[21] (Ezekiel 44: 9, KJV)

The biblical exclusion is cited numerous times in various Old Testament/Hebrew Bible passages.

> [16] And the LORD spake unto Moses, saying, [17] Speak unto Aaron, saying, Whosoever he be of thy seed in their generations that hath any blemish, let him not approach to offer the bread of his God. [18] For whatsoever man he be that hath a blemish, he shall not approach: a blind man, or a lame, or he that hath a flat nose, or any thing superfluous,[19] Or a man that is brokenfooted, or brokenhanded, [20] Or crookbackt, or a dwarf, or that hath a blemish in his eye, or be scurvy, or scabbed, or hath his stones broken;[21] No man that hath a blemish of the seed of Aaron the priest shall come nigh to offer the offerings of the LORD made by fire: he hath a blemish; he shall not come nigh to offer the bread of his God.[22] He shall eat the bread of his God, both of the most holy, and of the holy. [23] Only he shall not go in unto the vail, nor come nigh unto the altar, because he hath a blemish; that he profane not my sanctuaries: for I the LORD do sanctify them. [22] Leviticus 21: 16-23, KJV

It was well understood that certain men were forbidden from serving in the temple. This passage shifts previous understanding and teachings. Now, due to this revised teaching in Isaiah 56: 1-8, immigrants and eunuchs not only join the post exilic believers, eunuchs hold a special status. It is as if, because of the extraordinary societal or religions burden, they hold a special place in God's heart. God has always been a God of the oppressed, disenfranchised and outcast. While eunuchs held positions of influence in royal circles, their existence and activity were limited within the Jewish community of faith. Both Leviticus 21:16-23 and Deuteronomy 23:1-6 detail the strict restrictions.

---

[21]   Ezekiel 44:9, accessed on August 19, 2022, https://www.biblegateway.com/passage/?search=Ezekiel+44%3A9&version=KJV

[22]   Leviticus 21:16-23 King James Version, accessed August 19, 2022, https://www.biblegateway.com/passage/?search=Leviticus+21%3A+16-23&version=KJV

Another member of the exegetical review team, Karen W., shared the following:

> I have read Isaiah 56: 1-8 with great interest. It seems to speak directly to the issues of our day, as God is addressing all marginalized people. By "foreigners" and "eunuchs," I take it that God means people who regard themselves as somehow apart from God's chosen people, but more broadly, any person who feels different from others. Isaiah is reassuring those who feel doubtful that their piety, prayers, and observance of the Sabbath are welcome, that God welcomes them into His fold, just as He welcomed the Israelites. Their offerings and sacrifices are acceptable on God's altar. When Isaiah says, "I will gather yet others to him besides those already gathered," it is perhaps a prophecy that many Gentiles would soon be gathered to God, as the Israelites were. Who is present? Those who love God but feel like outcasts. Who is not? Those who already feel as if they are "God's people.[23]

Persons who don't fit the norm of the culture often experience alienation and exclusion both religiously and communally, even in our current times. In the United States of America, women, African Americans, and other racial ethnic minority individuals, have experienced various forms of exclusion within the nation and Christian community, especially related to church membership and the right to serve as ordained clergy. We now can add to the list of persons in question for inclusion in Christian faith communities, people of the LGBTQI community.[24] I wonder how this passage would be read today by a transgender individual, whose right to use the bathroom of his/her choice is part of the current national debate. In the United Methodist Church, the issue of homosexuality and the right of a "self-avowed and practicing" homosexual to serve as clergy, threatens to split the denomination. At the time of this writing, the Judicial Council was preparing to decide on the election of an openly married, lesbian bishop.

While for some, castration was not voluntary, for many families, it was desirable and even customary to select a son to live as a eunuch. Eunuchs

---

[23] Karen W. is a CUMC member who participated as part of the exegetical reflection group. Her response was received, by email, on March 15, 2017.

[24] LGBTQI Glossary, accessed on December 25, 2018, https://www.amnestyusa.org/pdfs/AIUSA_Pride2015Glossary.pdf.

occupied places of influence in the society, something that would benefit their families. On one hand, the status of a eunuch resulted in influence. On the other hand, the eunuch's status equaled a stigma in Judaism due to the inability to father children.

Children represent the continuation of a family name and serves as a legacy or monument. In the Hebrew society, children represent a memorial to their parents. The birth of a child gives witness to the "something" new God was doing. Families and even churches that fail to give birth are positioned to forfeit a memorial or legacy. It is through the future generations that the scriptures suggest, God's plan of salvation would come. The eunuch, without future generations, would be exempt from participating in God's future and on-going work of salvation. Today, churches have a role in ensuring God's salvation comes to future generations of all walks of life.

To live and die without a child signifies the end of a family. Children, especially males, held important roles in ancient Israelite families. "Boys and young men receive more attention from the Bible's writers than do girls. Sons were desired because ancient Israelite society was patrilocal, with the daughter moving to the house of her husband upon marriage. Although girls and women were valuable contributors to the labor of the household, a family without sons would be bereft of children to care for the parents in their old age."[25]

Without children, a eunuch would have no legacy. His name would end when his life did, unlike those who had children, namely sons, to carry their name for future generations. Heirs were important. Historical research suggests that some eunuchs adopted children.

In Jewish society, "When a man died without male offspring, to continue his line, his closest male relative was commanded to sleep with his widow and produce an heir."[26] The phrase, "don't let the eunuch say I'm only a dried up tree," speaks to the communal import of siring male children or having an

---

[25]   Julie Faith Parker, "Children in the Hebrew Bible," Bible Odyssey, accessed on March 16, 2017, https://www.bibleodyssey.org/en/passages/related-articles/children-in-the-hebrew-bible.

[26]   David Neff," Biblical Adoption is Not What You Think it Is," November 22, 2013, accessed on March 16, 2017, http://www.christianitytoday.com/ct/2013/december/heirs-biblicaliblical-take-on-adoption.html.

eternal inheritance through future generations. The dried up tree is incapable of reproduction. In this revised understanding, God will create and give the eunuch an inheritance even more special than children.

Isaiah 56: 3, 4, 5 & 7 appear to challenge or even nullify the previous Pentateuchal law related to eunuchs. What would cause God to change God's mind? Why does it appear that God now embraces a community of believers previously ostracized? In the case of eunuchs, the shift may not have affected an understanding of Pentateuchal law alone, but rather an acknowledgement that others, once outside of the circle have pledged their loyalty and fidelity to God, and thus obtained a special place in God's plan for the salvation of the nations.

It is noted that not everyone in the culture embraced the perspective of salvation for all. Some researchers provide additional insight.

> Isaiah 56–66 has often been associated with frustrated hopes for the restoration community, and thus with a return to a message of divine judgment after DI's message of comfort. In that light, it is somewhat surprising that TI has in recent years most often been taken up for a more uplifting aspect of its message: its call for inclusion of those previously excluded, notably foreigners (e.g., Croatto 1998; Flynn 2006; Gosse 2005; Hammock 2000). It is important to note, however, that a number of critical readings of the passages concerning the nations chasten readers from the notion that the latter portions of Isaiah are exuberantly universalistic (e.g., Croatto 2005; Kaminsky & Stewart 2006; Willis 1998).[27]

Wright and Chan's research sheds light on an ancient funeral practice of various cultures to create and inscribe commemorative memorials to honor the dead. Those would have been secured by family members, or as in the case of a eunuch, the family he served. It is their belief that the reference to memorial in the passage was related to funeral rites.

They assert that the change was not about Pentateuchal law but instead signified a shifted reality that more people, previously outside

---

27 Christopher B. Hayes, "The Book of Isaiah in Contemporary Research," *Religion Compass* accessed on March 31, 2017 (Hoboken, NJ: Blackwell Publishing 2011), 558. http://www.academia.edu/1883357/The_Book_of_Isaiah_in_Contemporary_Research.

the community of Israelite believers, were coming to faith in Adonai. "Therefore, if our text seeks to overrule or transform any-thing, it is not Pentateuchal law but imperial ideology," Wright and Chan explain. "YHWH'S promise to his faith-ful eunuchs turns a major symbol of royal power on its head by transferring absolute devotion to the empire, which eunuchs both symbolize and physically embody, to fidelity to YHWH."[28] In response to the eunuch's devotion, God would provide an eternal memorial, in the beloved temple of Jerusalem, as a witness of his love for God. The salvation that was promised was made relevant in the birth, life, death and resurrection of Jesus of Nazareth, whose very name means God is our Salvation.

What constitutes being part of God's kingdom? Does socio-economic standing or political party determine our connection to God? Does our gender provide Christ followers with an "admit one" ticket? In the current time this paper is being written, it appears to be a battle for devotion between political affiliation and God. Misplaced devotion can result in mistreatment of those whom God loves and sent God's Son to save. This passage reminds us that God's salvation is for everyone. Additionally, in this passage, God first addresses God's people so that they will live in right relationship with God and with others – foreigners and eunuchs.

> The opening and closing verses of vv.1-8 imply that the entire section addresses the Judahite community as a whole; the foreigner and eunuch are not the direct addressees...the prophet addresses the community as a whole with a view (among other things) to shaping its attitude to the foreigners and eunuchs in its midst.[29]

---

[28] Jacob L. Wright and Michael J. Chan, "King and Eunuch: Isaiah 56: 1-8 in light of Honorific Royal Burial Practices," *Journal of Biblical Literature*, 131, no. 1, 119, accessed March 28, 2017, http://web.a.ebscohost.com.utsdayton.idm.oclc.org/ehost/detail/detail?vid=7&sid=566d7b02-cb1f-4f22-845a-39589eaeeb6e%40sessionmgr4007&bdata=JnNpdGU9ZWhvc3QtbGl2ZQ%3d%3d#AN=ATLA0001886158&db=rfh

[29] John Goldingay "Isaiah 56: 1-8," *Isaiah 56-66 International Critical Commentary: A Critical and Exegetical Commentary.* London, England: Bloomsbury Publishing, 2014. 91, accessed February 5, 2018. http://dx.doi.org/10.5040/9781472556158.0008.

In the United States of America, the seeds of racism have permeated not just this nation but also Christian houses of worship. This passage challenges us to look beyond the differences and other issues with people identified as "other" so that people of faith can work to live out what it means to be God's multi-cultural, multi-ethnic, and multi-lingual family of believers. If God's salvation is for all, how can we exclude people from the love of a Christian faith community?

This pericope provides a sound biblical foundation for congregations to reach beyond themselves to share God's love with others. Congregations cannot shy away from sharing the good news of the gospel with others who do not share their gender, socio-economic standing, culture, language, or color. God's salvation is for all. It is time to build bridges with the diverse communities in which we find ourselves. The congregation I pastor serves as a meeting place for a myriad of community organizations. This passage reminds us that it is not enough for people to meet in our church buildings yet remain disconnected from God and ministry with God's people. Like the ben-naker of the Isaiah 56 text, the people who meet in the building are those who are on the periphery of the church's ministry. God wants those who come on the premises to become a part of the worshipping community.

NEW TESTAMENT

Acts 10:44-48 New International Version (NIV)

[44] While Peter was still speaking these words, the Holy Spirit came on all who heard the message. [45] The circumcised believers who had come with Peter were astonished that the gift of the Holy Spirit had been poured out even on Gentiles. [46] For they heard them speaking in tongues[a] and praising God. Then Peter said, [47] "Surely no one can stand in the way of their being baptized with water. They have received the Holy Spirit just as we have." [48] So he ordered that they be baptized in the name of Jesus Christ. Then they asked Peter to stay with them for a few days.[30]

---

[30] Acts: 10: 44-48, accessed December 5, 2017, https://www.biblegateway.com/passage/?search=Acts+10%3A+44-48&version=NIV.

Authored by Luke the physician, researchers offer different dates for the time of writing. Some contend that the book of the Acts of the Apostles was written sometime during A.C.E. 55 and 59, while others suggest that it was written in A.C.E. 70, "after the destruction of Jerusalem." [31] Like the Isaiah 56: 1-8 passage, these scriptures test or push the boundaries of inclusion and exclusion within the community of believers. Contrasted with the Old Testament passage, this one challenges the new community or sect of Christ followers now within Jewish believers. These Jewish believers adhered to the teachings of the Law, related to food and human interactions in reference to purity or impurity. Observance of the Sabbath and adherence to circumcision were important.

As Jewish followers of Jesus they believed he was the one who fulfilled the Messianic prophetic promises of old. Jesus of Nazareth was the promised Messiah who would restore Israel to power. As this passage illustrates, the question of belonging or not belonging, inclusion versus exclusion, will ultimately define the early Christian church. Even though there existed numerous instances in the Old Testament that gave witness to God's ultimate plan for the salvation for everyone, the issue of Gentile inclusion is initially problematic.

It is interesting that our passage inaugurates the tension in this nascent community through the involvement of the disciple, now apostle, Simon Peter. Our passage is part of a larger pericope which spans Acts 9: 32-11:30. As one commentator explained, this larger movement recounts the gospel movement through the "ever-widening circle,"[32] from Jerusalem, to Judea, Samaria and beyond. The components of this larger passage are identified as follows:

Acts 9: 32-43 Peter Heals Aeneas and Raises Tabitha from death
Acts 10: 1-8 Cornelius has a divine visitation
Acts 10: 9-16 Peter has a divine vision
Acts 10: 17-23a Peter welcomes Cornelius' Messengers

---

[31]   Carl R. Holladay, "Acts," *Harper's Bible Commentary.* (San Francisco: Harper San Francisco, 1988), 1077

[32]   In his book, *Preaching for Church Transformation*, Bill Easum uses the phrase "the ever-widening circle" to explain the move of the gospel from Jerusalem, Judea, Samaria and beyond. (Nashville, TN: Abingdon Press, 2010).

Acts 10:23b-33 The Meeting of Peter and Cornelius

Acts 10:34-43 Peter's Sermon

Acts 10: 44-48 Gentiles are accepted

Acts 11: 1-18 Peter Justifies his Ministry with Gentiles

Acts 11: 19-30 Christianity arrives in Antioch[33]

Simon's new name from Jesus gives us an indication of his role establishing and communicating the foundation of this new faith community. Simon is the Rock, as his new name, Peter, or Petra, communicates. It is Peter whom God will first use to demonstrate that God's new community of believers will include Jew and Gentile. Both Jews and Gentiles are legitimately part of the faith community. There is no distinction in God's ultimate salvation plan. It has always been God's ultimate plan, yet it is through this apostle that this message is made clearer. It is through this passage that a bridge is made between the Jewish Christians and new Gentile Christians.

As we engage this passage, it is important to read and digest it from the worldview of the original intended community and author. We can and do not inherently understand the cultural, sociological, and religious reality of people who lived more than 2,000 years ago. "The problem for us modern readers is that these texts and their social systems are alien to us. In order to get a glimpse of what these texts possibly mean, we have to fill in the gaps and read between the lines."[34] Any biases and limited understanding inhibit our understanding of the nuances of what was happening as salvation was bridging the gap from Jewish to Jewish Christians and to Gentiles.

More detailed research indicates that Simon Peter bridged other societal differences before breaking the Jewish-Gentile divide. Among the rules adhered to by Jews were those relating to that which was clean or unclean. When summoned by Cornelius the Centurion, a Gentile,

---

[33] Carl R. Holladay, "Acts," *Harper's Bible Commentary*, (San Francisco, CA: Harper San Francisco, 1988), 1092-1094.

[34] Van Thanh Nguyen, SVD, "Dismantling Cultural Boundaries, Missiological Implications of Acts 10:1-11:18," *Missiology An International Review*, Vol XL, no 4, October 2012, 455, Accessed December 5, 2017. http://web.a.ebscohost.com. utsdayton.idm.oclc.org/ehost/pdfviewer/pdfviewer?vid=1&sid=1afedd51-fd1e-47b5-802c-a63447cb0942%40sessionmgr4006.

Peter was staying in the house of Simon the tanner, vs. 6 & 32, a person considered ritually unclean by the law. "Thus, Peter's decision to reside in the house of Simon the tanner reveals that the apostle is receptive to Jews who are considered marginalized and unclean."[35] Simon the tanner's marginalization is due to his interaction with dead animals. Work with dead animals caused him to be deemed unclean. It was this person, deemed ritually unclean by Jewish law, whom Simon Peter decided to stay.

Like the Isaiah passage, in the midst of the larger Acts passage, we encounter Gentiles who too loved God and adhered, as converted Jewish believers, to faith in God. Cornelius, a Gentile Centurion, his household and even a member of his cohort are identified as having faith in God and are probably converts to Judaism.

An angel visits Cornelius to inform him that his alms and prayers have been received as a memorial before God and that he should have Peter visit him so that he can hear what Peter has to say. As Cornelius' workers are in route to connect with the apostle, Peter has a divine encounter of his own. Hungry, on the roof for his midday prayer, Peter sees three visions in which a sheet containing a mixture of clean and unclean animals are lowered to his presence, as provision for him to satisfy his need to eat. Three times, God had to tell Peter to override his previous understanding of what was unclean and to eat from what was lowered before him. Leviticus 11 provides an in-depth understanding of the potential revulsion Peter had to overcome related to food in order to go and stay in the home of a Gentile.

Could it have been that through Peter's encounter with Cornelius and the vision of food once identified as unclean, yet now clean, God was again giving witness to God's original plan before the fall, as some commentators suggest? All of creation was good at the beginning. Brokenness among relationships and disunity among animals and sin were introduced through the fall. God is no respecter of persons.

All of this sets the stage for more barriers and boundaries to be eliminated. Food served as a social barrier among Jews, Christians, and

---

[35] Van Thanh Nguyen, SVD, "Dismantling Cultural Boundaries, Missiological Implications of Acts 10:1-11:18," *Missiology An International Review*, Vol XL, no 4, October 2012, 455, Accessed December 5, 2017. http://web.a.ebscohost.com. utsdayton.idm.oclc.org/ehost/pdfviewer/pdfviewer?vid=1&sid=1afedd51-fd1e-47b5-802c-a63447cb0942%40sessionmgr4006.

pagans. "Food-related customs connected those who shared them and confirmed their identities as individuals and as a collectivity. At the same time, restrictions concerning what could be eaten, with whom, and under what conditions strongly influenced the social interaction of various religious groups in Hellenistic and Roman society."[36]

Societal and religious barriers and boundaries were stretched and dismantled as people shared meals together. Jesus tested those barriers and boundaries when he ate with sinners and lepers (Mark 2: 13-17). Jewish society deemed them as unclean. Jesus mingled with individuals who were shunned and found outside the norm of respectable society. Jesus also shared that all food was clean, (Mark 7:19). The mores about Jewish-Gentile interactions were problematic for the early Christian community. Peter had to overcome these issues to be in ministry with the growing circle of Christian believers.

> The passage highlights the debate which existed among believers about food, whether it is clean or unclean. "In sum: we see continuous debate concerning the applicability of Jewish dietary law and concerning commensality with outsiders."[37] Everyone did not share the same opinion. "The authors of the Gospels of Mark, Matthew and Luke (and *Acts* 10) took sides in this debate, by stressing that Jesus and/or God himself had said that all food was clean."[38] Nonetheless, the risk that Peter takes breaking these codes, cannot be ignored. "[28] And he said unto them, Ye know how that it is an unlawful thing for a man that is a Jew to keep company, or come unto one of another nation; but God hath shewed me that I should not call any man common or unclean. [29] Therefore came I unto you without gainsaying, as soon as I was sent for: I ask therefore for what intent ye have sent for me?"[39] Acts 10:28-29, KJV

---

[36] Paul Erdkamp's, "Jews and Christians at the Dinner Table: A Study in Social and Religious Interaction," *Food & History*, vol. 9, (Brussel: Belgium, Vakgroep Geschiedenis, Vrije Universiteit, 2012), 100.

[37] Erdkamp's, "Jews and Christians at the Dinner Table: A Study in Social and Religious Interaction," *Food & History*, vol. 9. 100.

[38] Erdkamp's, "Jews and Christians at the Dinner Table: A Study in Social and Religious Interaction," *Food & History*, vol. 9, 100.

[39] Acts 10: 28-29, New International Version, Bible Gateway, accessed October 3, 2022, https://www.biblegateway.com/passage/?search=Acts+10%3A+28-29&version=KJV

The Holy Spirit continues to address issues of inclusion and exclusion and dismantle the barriers. In the passage preceding Acts 10: 44-48, Peter shares the story of the gospel in the midst of Cornelius, the Centurion, his friends, and family. Also, present are Jewish male followers of Jesus, identified as circumcised believers." Not particular to Jews only, "the removal of the foreskin (prepuce) of the male penis,"[40]circumcision was practiced by others including the Ammonites, Egyptians, Edomites, Moabites and Arabs. The difference was that for Jews, circumcision represented a sign of God's covenant with them.

The identification of circumcised believers, present with Peter, continues the literary tension of Jewish vs. Gentile believer. God's salvation is available for all and therefore others are invited into God's covenant. Covenant relationship with God extends beyond the physical markings of circumcision to the spiritual markings of the heart. Gentile and Jewish believers witness the move of God affirming salvation to all nations and peoples, through Jesus Christ. It is one thing for clergy to grasp this understanding. If laity do not grasp this understanding of God's salvation being for everyone, church transformation and revitalization efforts can be difficult. In fact, if not understood as God's ultimate plan, some may fight efforts to share in ministry with people deemed previously as "other," "inferior" and "unwanted." Larry and Joyce W., of my exegetical reflection group, added the following insights in response to Acts 10:44-48.

> Although these words are wonderful, we do not believe that they have expressed the mainstream of Jewish thought down through the ages. Generally, Judaism has been not interested in evangelism and has been content to remain the religion of a particular people rather than a religion for the whole world. However, the Jews have often been a "light to the nations" through the ideas and practices that their religion has introduced. The fact that Jewish synagogues in the time of Jesus were sometimes frequented by Gentile "God fearers" indicates the interest in Judaism by the broader world. However, there was a problem for the spread of Judaism: the legalism of its approach, the great concern for scrupulous adherence to the covenant laws and many derived

---

[40] Paul J. Achtemeier, *Harper's Bible Dictionary*, (San Francisco, CA: Harper Collins, 1985), 170.

interpretations made it unlikely that Judaism could spread in its present form to become a world religion. However, in its "mutated" form via Paul and other early Christian writers/ believers, it could and did. [41]

Wind moves where it wills. The same is even truer with the Holy Spirit. The Holy Spirit goes where it wants. This passage is reminiscent of the promised outpouring of the Holy Spirit on all flesh (Joel 2:28 and Acts 2:17). This passage also provides a contrast to the building of the Tower of Babel where people were first separated by languages (Genesis 11: 1-9). In the presence of Cornelius, and a host of Gentiles, the Spirit crosses boundaries and eliminates barriers that once separated people.

As Peter speaks about salvation through Jesus Christ, the Holy Spirit descends upon the Gentiles as evidenced by the speaking in "unknown tongues," γλῶσσα glossa[42]. Individuals upon whom the Holy Spirit descended began to speak languages they had not previously learned, an experience of Jewish Christians which began during Pentecost after the resurrection of Jesus Christ. Through both the Jewish and Gentile Christians God further fulfilled the prophetic promised outpouring of God's Spirit on all flesh.

The Jewish festival of Pentecost, also known as Shavuot or Festival of Weeks, commemorated God's giving of the Law to Moses on Mt. Sinai and the last of the grain harvests. It was a time through which Jews obtained a special designation as God's chosen, set apart, and called people – people charged with being a light of God's power to other nations. Similarly, the Jewish and Gentile recipients of the Holy Spirit's Pentecost experience received a new identity as God's ambassadors of reconciliation, love, healing, and power in the earth. [43]

God's plan to offer salvation to the entire world, moves forth. Salvation will not be determined or maintained by human constraints, as evidenced by the experience. The Greek expression for Holy Spirit, in the Acts 10:

---

[41]   Responses from Larry and Joyce W., members of the Cheverly UMC Exegetical Study Group. Shared March 23, 2017, in an email.

[42]   Glossa, γλῶσσα, Strong's Concordance, 1100, accessed on March 30, 2017. http://biblehub.com/greek/1100.htm.

[43]   Feast of Pentecost, accessed on February 19, 2018, https://www.thoughtco.com/feast-of-pentecost-700186.

44,45,47, is ἅγιος, hagios, which denotes sacred or consecrated. Could it be that God's initial plan of creation was being restored? Humanity's sin, spiritual death, broken relationship between God and others, and creation resulted from the fall. Things are being renewed and restored. That which had experienced God's Holy Spirit is once again available to all who want to live that Kingdom reality now. Again, images of the Tower of Babel are evoked for this writer, as now, people of different ethnos are connected by heavenly languages instead of being separated by earthly languages. These individuals now join together in magnifying God's greatness in new unlearned languages they don't understand.

In Acts 10:44-48, Jew and Gentile are together, as Peter shares the gospel. As an indication of the impartiality of God, the Holy Spirit descends and is poured on the Gentile believers, in the presence of the Jewish believers. Gentiles, defined as ethnos, ἔθνος, represents various nations and peoples. Reflections from the exegetical study group members shared similar perspectives.

> This passage talks about Peter's amazement that the Holy Spirit has fallen upon Gentiles who heard the word and his following argument that "Can anyone forbid water for baptizing these people who have received the Holy Spirit just as we have?" Thus, Peter is saying that these Gentiles should be baptized and added to the circle of believers. This is one of a number of statements in Acts (and also in the Pauline and other NT letters) which state the Christian position rather than the Jewish position that the Holy Spirit (and inclusion in the faith) is available to all who hear and respond to the word. It is hard to quarrel with this since we both grew up in this belief. However, we think that the fairest statement about this is that Jewish people in general would not agree with this type of inclusivity and that the Old Testament is far more concerned with the Jews remaining faithful to the covenant, part of which was involved not worshipping non-Jewish gods or following non-Jewish customs or beliefs. We were pleased that verse 48 of Acts 10 mentions that the people wish Peter to stay with them longer. This seems to show that the people wanted to learn more about this inclusive Christian way of life."[44]

---

[44] Responses from Larry and Joyce W., members of the Cheverly UMC Exegetical Study Group. Shared March 23, 2017, in an email.

Baptism in the early Christian church had strong connections with its Jewish roots. We find evidence of this reality through the baptisms performed by John the Baptist in the Jordan River. Not only did John baptize Jesus and but other Jews as well.

> In Judaism, baptism was a means of purification. Washing primarily fulfilled the legal requirements of ritual purity so that Jews could sacrifice at the Temple. Later, as "God-fearers" or "righteous" Gentiles expressed their desire to convert to Judaism, priests broadened the rite's meaning, and along with circumcision, performed baptism as a sign of the covenant given to Abraham. [45]

Gentile converts to Judaism would also undergo baptism and males, circumcision, to become part of God's covenant people. It would only make sense that Jewish Christians would expect Gentile Christians to complete some actions in order to become part of the worshipping community. Peter assures the "circumcised believers," that the new Gentile believers should be baptized because of the Holy Spirit's presence in a manner reminiscent of the experience of early Jewish Christians. The Christian understanding of baptism is different though. Baptism is to the Christian what circumcision is to the Jewish male believer. For the Christian believer, baptism signifies the transition from death to life/resurrection and sin to forgiveness/repentance.

In Acts 10:44-48, Jew and Gentile are together, as Peter shares the gospel. As an indication of the overarching love of God for all people, the Holy Spirit descends and is poured on the Gentile believers, in the presence of the Jewish believers. In the times and locations in which we live, it is important to identify what God is doing and wants to do through us individually and congregationally. The Holy Spirit's action, once again, as evidenced in the Isaiah text, radically challenges the Christian community's understanding of inclusion. Gentiles, considered as unclean, are recipients of The Holy Spirit. "To the *amazement* of Peter's company of circumcised Jews, upon these *Gentiles*-uncircumcised and unclean-the *Holy Spirit* was

---

[45] Stephen Gertz, "What is the pre-Christian history of the baptismal ceremony?" Christianity Today. Posted August 8, 2008, accessed on April 2017, http://www.christianitytoday.com/history/2008/august/what-is-pre-christian-history-of-baptismal-ceremony.html.

poured out, immediately from heaven."[46] God is not confined to human understanding or social barriers. "It proves that God is free, and that his grace is not confined to any channels."[47] God's action represents a seismic shift among Jewish Christians. Gentiles now too experienced that which took place that first Pentecost after the resurrection of Jesus Christ. "Gentile Pentecost was clear evidence that the blessing of God was upon Gentiles as much as upon Jews."[48] It is interesting to note that in this text God shifts the way things are done. Prior to this pericope, baptism of the believer was associated with the gift of the Holy Spirit. Now, the Holy Spirit is given freely apart from baptism. "Here uniquely, except for the Jewish Pentecost, the Spirit is given independently and unmediated. Baptism now follows as the mark of the full incorporation of Gentiles into the New Israel."[49]

Each congregation praying and yearning for renewal would benefit from a Pentecost experience. It will only be through the Holy Spirit's power that every local church will be able to fulfill its true call to make disciples in and beyond its zip code. On its own, a congregation is helpless and does not have the power to fulfill God's call.

> The Holy Spirit is given freely as a gift to enable disciples to enter into a new life of intimacy with and obedience to God. Obedience in Acts begins with the helpless, waiting: the disciples are helpless in the sense that they were told that on their own, they have no power. They needed to be empowered for whatever service or call God would send them to do.[50]

Congregations would do well to follow the teachings presented in both scriptures. In order to meet the challenge, people will need to first pray, seek God, and then listen to what God is saying related to God's will for the congregation in the community. The next step is to follow the leading of

---

[46] Richard Belward Rackham. *The Acts of the Apostles.* (London, England: Methuen & Co. Ltd. 1925), 159.

[47] Rackham. *The Acts of the Apostles,* 159.

[48] William Neil, *The Acts of the Apostles.* (London, England: Oliphants. 1973), 141.

[49] Neil, *The Acts of the Apostles,* 141.

[50] Musimbi Kanyoro, "Thinking Mission in Africa," *A Feminist Companion to the Acts of the Apostles,* ed. Amy-Jill Levine and Marianne Blickenstaff (London, England: T & T Clark International 2004), 63.

the Holy Spirit. That is not always easy and requires an openness to getting outside of comfort zones and entering into sometimes unknown situations. It requires being willing to love others who are outside the congregation.

In both the Hebrew and Christian Bible texts, God directed God's people to reach beyond those already present or engaged in the community. In both of the biblical passages addressed in this book, God sent the people of faith to interact and share in ministry with people who fit in the previous societal and/or religious category of "personas non-grata." What are the implications for us today?

Our stories start off with God as the Savior of only the Jews. In that manner God had demonstrated a partiality towards the children of Jacob. While it first appears that God is in some ways partial only to Jewish believers, God changes to be impartial to everyone who loves God – including the Jewish Christians, and then to Gentile believers. God's ultimate desire and design is for all people to be in loving relationship with God and each other. Of course, that is easier said than done, as evidenced by heightened levels of racism, sexism, and other prejudices confronting this society.

At the time of this book's writing, I served as pastor of Cheverly United Methodist Church, "the church in the heart of the community with the community in its heart." The congregation is centrally located and has earned goodwill among neighbors. The congregation would benefit by bridging the divides existing between it and its neighbors. Those divides include generational, linguistic, socio-economic, cultural/racial, and increasingly sexual orientation. Rooted in an evangelical heritage, CUMC would benefit from again intentionally engaging others with the good news of Jesus Christ and not be surprised how the Holy Spirit moves. God is no respecter of persons. CUMC has already navigated the shift from its inception as a homogenous, all Anglo-American congregation, to a mixed or multi-cultural congregation. Just as Peter had a vision that prompted him to go with Cornelius' workers, we have the option of embracing God's vision for the neighbors or those who are outside the church. Cheverly UMC's experience mirrors many other congregations.

Inherent in the process of bridge building between congregations and their surrounding neighborhoods is the fulfilled call of Christ followers. Members growing in faith formation are equipped to live their God assignment as disciples. Why share your faith with someone if you don't believe it is important? How does one live as a disciple if you don't know what it entails? When Christian believers do not grow in faith formation, they reflect the culture instead of the countercultural nature of God's kingdom. Only when we understand that we share our faith because that is what Jesus commissioned us to do, will we live out the assignment.

Some have identified our challenge as a "discipleship deficit."[51] Discipleship is a lifestyle, which appears to be missing in plain sight in many congregations. Modern day disciples often don't know what they have been called to do. The following have been identified as the seven marks of discipleship by Greg Ogden:

1. Proactive Ministers
2. A Disciplined Way of Life
3. Discipleship Affects all of Life
4. A Countercultural Force
5. An Essential, Chosen Organism
6. Biblically Informed People
7. People Who Share Their Faith [52]

In all of this, it is important for congregations to be a part of what God is doing and not the other way around. God is always on the move. Our challenge and opportunity is to be a part of what God is doing instead of asking God to bless what we are doing. God's way brings better results. If Peter had not heeded the vision, he would have missed an opportunity that ultimately transformed the spread of Christianity in the world. If we don't heed God's call for this present age, congregations will miss participating in God's transformation of individuals, families, and neighborhoods.

Re-Establish the Root Connection

Disciples make disciples. Strengthening the disciple-making system will strengthen the congregation's kingdom building. Only in connection

---

51 Greg Ogden, "The Discipleship Deficit: Where Have All the Disciples Gone?" Knowing & Doing, C.S. Lewis Institute, 2011, accessed on April 2, 2017, http://www.cslewisinstitute.org/The_Discipleship_Deficit_SinglePage.

52 Greg Ogden, "The Discipleship Deficit: Where Have All the Disciples Gone?"

with God can congregants connect with community members and facilitate the development of relationships and ministry to and with the community.

The imperatives needed for this effort are:

1. Reclamation of God's Kingdom Mandate in the community
2. Renewed and strengthened relationship with God – Father, Son and Holy Spirit.
3. Engaging the community
4. Getting past the fear of sharing one's faith
5. Standing for one's faith
6. Being in relationship with others outside the church
7. Embracing a Christian understanding of what it means to be in ministry with the community.
8. Following the direction of and yielding to the Holy Spirit

Each imperative would enhance disciple-making that could transform Christ-followers and persons outside of the local church. This approach can address spiritual amnesia and the loss of missional awareness in many contemporary mainline congregations. God has a desire to shower love on people beyond the church walls. Where is the Holy Spirit leading us today? Will we be a part of what God is doing?

THREE

Historical Foundations

———— ❧ ————

William J. Seymour and the Azusa Street Revival

Racism Hinders Multiethnic, Multicultural Ministry

THE LEGACY OF RACISM IN the United States has long impacted all aspects of life, including churches. Congregations in the United States have, historically and in many instances, been comprised primarily of one cultural or racial population group. This reality exists in a country context where American Christians represent a variety of cultural, ethnic, and racial groups.

During the 1960s, Dr. Martin Luther King, Jr. often lamented the segregation that existed in Christian churches. He rightly believed that Christian worship services and churches should have reflected ethnic and cultural diversity more than any other component of society. Why wouldn't Christians follow the example of Jesus Christ in His love for people of various ethnicities and cultures? Sadly to say, his observation is still true today in many place.

Segregated worship is still a challenging reality at the time this writing, years after Dr. King's famous observation. It was the case during the Azusa Street Revival, which took place from 1906 to 1909. The spiritual movement began after the turn of the century, four years after the end of the Spanish-American War, and forty years after the end of U.S. slavery. The country was balancing the euphoria from successful imperialistic wars and conquests in Asian lands and territory with racial tensions between

European Americans and non-European Americans at home. It can accurately be said that racism was par for the course at that time.

Descendants of former slaves and slave owners were adjusting to life after emancipation. During this time period, the United States developed a sense of national pride and implemented efforts to live out their perceived God-given assignment to conquer and "save" people in other countries. An example of this sentiment is reflected in Rudyard Kipling's poem, "The White Man's Burden."

> Take up the White Man's burden—
> Send forth the best ye breed—
> Go send your sons to exile
> To serve your captives' need
> To wait in heavy harness
> On fluttered folk and wild—
> Your new-caught, sullen peoples,
> Half devil and half child[53]

President William McKinley's words appeared to embrace beliefs scribed in the aforementioned poem, referring to the U.S.'s annexation of the Philippines after the Spanish-American War of 1898. "By annexing the Philippines, the United States took up the so-called 'White Man's Burden,' as urged by poet Rudyard Kipling. It would be our purpose," said McKinley, "to take them all and to educate the Filipinos, and uplift and civilize and Christianize them."[54] McKinley was not alone in this perspective. There existed a prevalent belief that people needed to be helped or saved. "General Governor William Howard Taft, said, 'They are our little brown brothers,'"[55] in reference to the Filipinos.

---

[53] "History Matters: The US Survey Course on the Web," accessed May 10, 2017, http://historymatters.gmu.edu/d/5478/.

[54] Library of Congress, "America at the Turn of the Century: A Look at the Historical Context," Washington, D.C., accessed May 10, 2017, https://www.loc.gov/collections/early-films-of-new-york-1898-to-1906/articles-and-essays/america-at-the-turn-of-the-century-a-look-at-the-historical-context/.

[55] Library of Congress, "America at the Turn of the Century: A Look at the Historical Context."

How could a multiethnic or multiracial revival break out during a time of such upheaval, amidst such racism? How did God move among people of diverse cultures, colors, and socio-economic backgrounds to birth a spiritual awakening that changed the face of church life on the global stage and challenged the societal norms of that time? Yet that is exactly what God did in the 1906 to 1909 Azusa Street Revival of Los Angeles, California. During this movement, people of diverse ethnicities and cultures participated in the ministry. Hispanics, African Americans, Asians, and European Americans worshipped, prayed, and worked together for God's Kingdom. The color line was greatly challenged during this brief period. What can we learn from the Christian ministry during this time?

In this chapter, I will focus my study on the Azusa Street Revival of 1906 to 1909 and its leader, the Rev. William Joseph Seymour. During the days of Jim Crow, the Azusa Street Revival bridged racial, gender, socio-economic, and denominational lines, and attracted a multiethnic body of believers. My research will analyze the Azusa Street Revival, focus attention on Seymour's leadership, and identify insights relevant to our current context. The Azusa Street Revival propelled the Pentecostal movement to new heights across the United States and the globe. The Azusa Street Revival provides congregations with insights that will help them more effectively bridge the divide and minister to their multiethnic neighbors or within their multiethnic communities.

Disciple making in many congregations has diminished, which has been caused by and resulted in a loss of understanding of the mission of the church and a low priority for reaching new people for Christ, despite the fact that many churches are surrounded by myriads of people. Congregational ministry must grow to include disciple making for those who are already a part of the worshipping community, those whom God brings in the building and those who live in the surrounding neighborhood. Disciples make disciples. Strengthening the disciple making system will strengthen the congregation's Kingdom-building. Through creating or enhancing disciple making systems disciples will be invited to create a bridge by which congregants can connect with community members and facilitate the development of relationships and ministry to and with the community. Bridge-building is especially necessary so that the congregation can more effectively reach neighbors in their socio-economically and ethnically, racially, and culturally diverse community, with the transforming love of Jesus Christ.

The Holy Spirit Transcended Barriers to Birth Revival

In hindsight, the issue of racism should have prevented this move of God from taking place. There is no logical reason that can be used to explain how Azusa Street took place. Racism should have derailed it. Racism is often defined as prejudice plus power. *The Merriam-Webster Dictionary* defines racism as:

1. a belief that race is the primary determinant of human traits and capacities
2. and that racial differences produce an inherent superiority of a particular race
3. a doctrine or political program based on the assumption of racism and designed to execute its principles
4. a political or social system founded on racism[56]

The revival was birthed in a time of institutional, systematic, and legalized racism. Racism not only influences how people view themselves, but also how they view others, impacting everyone involved. How did society view a soft-spoken, southern-born African American man who was blind in one eye? By and large, African American males were not viewed favorably, especially in the leadership of a multiethnic context.

The foremost leader in this movement was William James Seymour. Born one of eleven children on May 2, 1870, in Centerville, Louisiana, to former slaves Simon Seymour and Phillis Salabar Seymour, Simon served as a soldier in the Union Army's 25th Regiment Infantry.[57] The 25th Regiment Infantry was later named the 93rd Regimental Infantry, United

---

[56] Merriam-Webster.com, accessed May 22, 2017, https://www.merriam-webster.com/dictionary/racism.

[57] Larry Martin, *The Life and Ministry of William J. Seymour* (Joplin, MO: Christian Life Books, 1999), 49.

States Colored Troops.[58] U.S. Census and baptismal records indicate that William was one of a few siblings who lived to adulthood.[59] As was typical of that era, the Seymour family dealt with abject poverty.[60]

According to various accounts, Seymour had the benefit of formal education. While William's formal education resulted in his ability to read, he reportedly was used by God to spark a spiritual revival that covered the globe. A man of deep faith, he was known to experience dreams and visions.[61]

His religious background interfaced with various Christian traditions including Roman Catholic, Baptist, Methodist Episcopal, and Holiness. Some reports assert that he was born into a family with "a long Roman Catholic," tradition, and that his mother was a member of a Baptist Church.[62] As an adult, he joined the Simpson Chapel Methodist Episcopal Church in Indianapolis, Indiana. Differing information exists about Simpson Chapel ME Church.[63] Some researchers contend that the church was an African American worshiping community, yet part of a racially diverse denomination. Other research suggests that, at the time Seymour joined Simpson Chapel, it was a racially mixed congregation that later experienced segregation. In any event, research indicates the Methodist Episcopal Church "had a strong evangelistic outreach to all classes and races."[64] The Methodist Episcopal Church's evangelistic outreach to people of all races assuredly influenced, or at least built upon, Seymour's dream for a multiethnic community of faith. Seymour was also influenced by

---

[58] Martin, *The Life and Ministry of William J. Seymour,* 50.

[59] Martin, *The Life and Ministry of William J. Seymour,* 54-55.

[60] Encyclopedia of World Biography, "William Joseph Seymour," accessed December 27, 2017, http://www.notablebiographies.com/supp/Supplement-Mi-So/Seymour-William-Joseph.html.

[61] Encyclopedia of World Biography, "William Joseph Seymour."

[62] Erik J. Hjalmeby, "A Rhetorical History of Race Relations in the Early Pentecostal Movement, 1906-1916," (Waco, TX: M.A. thesis, Baylor University, 2007), 40, accessed December 27, 2017, https://baylor-ir.tdl.org/baylor-ir/bitstream/handle/2104/5062/erik_hjalmeby_masters.pdf?sequence=1.

[63] Hjalmeby, "A Rhetorical History of Race Relations in the Early Pentecostal Movement, 1906-1916," 41.

[64] Roberts Liardon, "God's Generals: William Seymour," accessed May 15, 2017, godsgenerals.com.

the "Evening Light Saints," a group in Indianapolis, Indiana. Seymour's attraction to this group no doubt was due to their adherence to the equal treatment of whites and blacks. "In the 1890s the Evening Light Saints was one of the few groups in which whites and blacks were treated equally and gifted women were encouraged to preach."[65]

As in other parts of the country, the racial divides were increasing in Indianapolis. Seymour later moved to Cincinnati, Ohio, "to pursue his dream of cross-racial ministry."[66] This approach to ministry was both counterintuitive and countercultural in a country struggling with racial tension. What would cause Seymour to think that cross-racial ministry was possible during his day? While the influence of the Evening Lights Saints left an indelible mark on his approach to ministry related to racial equality, so did the early Methodist teaching about the grace of God for all people regardless of race, culture, or ethnicity. His belief that all people were equal in God's eyes and his desire for racial harmony became bedrocks of his ministry.

The Pentecostal movement, from which the Azusa Street Revival hails, descends itself from the Methodist and Holiness Movements. While there are stark differences, the Methodist and Holiness movements have strong similarities and connections including sanctification and a belief that the movement was sent by God to transform the region, the nation, and the world.

Sanctification, a tenet of Methodism, was embraced by the Pentecostals, who built upon and enlarged the original Methodist understanding. "The belief in everyday leading by the Spirit is the most obvious connection between the original Methodist Revival and the later explosion of modern Pentecostalism."[67] Some of the outward manifestations of the Holy Spirit exhibited in the early Pentecostal movement were also part of the early Methodist movement, including: "shaking, being slain in the spirit, then identified as passing out, and enthusiastic speech."[68] "Another similarity

---

[65] Cecil M. Robeck Jr., *The Azusa Street Mission and Revival: The Birth of the Global Pentecostal Movement* (Nashville, TN: Thomas Nelson Publishers, 2006), 30.

[66] Roberts Liardon, "God's Generals: William Seymour," accessed May 16, 2017, godsgenerals.com.

[67] Robert R. Owens, *Speak to the Rock: The Azusa Street Revival.* (Lanham, MD: University Press of America, 1998), 24.

[68] Owens, *Speak to the Rock: The Azusa Street Revival.* Owens referenced research by Arthur Wilford Nagler, "The Church in History," 183-194.

is apparent in the many reports of ecstatic reactions of the people who flocked to the meetings."[69] In both movements, people prayed for an outpouring of God's Spirit, so that lives and communities would be changed. The ties that bound their Methodist forebears and Holiness and Pentecostal branches of the family eventually caused the birth of new denominations, like the Pentecostal Church of the Nazarene. Started in 1895, this denomination was founded by a former Methodist Episcopal, M.E., Pastor, Phineas F. Bresee. After his bishop instructed him to halt the church's ministry with the poor, Bresee left the M.E. church and founded the Church of the Nazarene.

The understanding of sanctification was a major point of contention among the Methodists, the Holiness Movement, and the Pentecostals. All agreed that sanctification was the work of the Holy Spirit through which the new believer was made holy or set apart unto the Lord. John Wesley believed and taught on "entire sanctification." For Wesley, "sanctification began after our pardoning through justification." In his sermon, "The Scripture Way of Salvation," he explained:

> In that instant we are born again, born from above, born of the Spirit: there is a real as well as a relative change. We are inwardly renewed by the power of God. We feel "the love of God shed abroad in our heart by the Holy Ghost which is given unto us"; producing love to all mankind, and more especially to the children of God; expelling the love of the world."[70]

Wesley believed that sanctification began instantaneously, and that sin's hold on us was destroyed immediately, but that the work of sanctification was also ongoing. Wesley contended that, with the new birth, a person begins the lifelong process of being made in the image of Christ.

For the offspring of Methodism, sanctification for Pentecostals included the baptism of the Holy Spirit as evidenced by speaking in tongues. In fact, the baptism of the Holy Spirit through speaking in tongues was a required

---

[69]   Owens, *Speak to the Rock: The Azusa Street Revival.*

[70]   Wesley Center for Applied Theology, "The Scripture Way of Salvation," Wesley Center Online, Northwest Nazarene University, 1999, accessed May 24, 2017, http://wesley.nnu.edu/john-wesley/the-sermons-of-john-wesley-1872-edition/sermon-43-the-scripture-way-of-salvation/.

and expected sign of sanctification in Pentecostalism. The baptism of the Holy Spirit was not only accompanied by speaking in unknown tongues, but also the gifts of the spirit. Historical accounts indicate the presence of the gifts of the spirit in the Methodist movement. Again, another similarity exists between the early Methodist and Pentecostal movements. Some sources identify the presence of all of the gifts of the spirit except one existed in the Methodist movement. "One study has shown that, 'a careful study of Wesley's *Works* and particularly of the lives of the early Methodist preachers reveals evidence that all the spiritual gifts listed in 1 Corinthians 12:8-10 were exercised, with the one exception of the interpretation of tongues.'"[71] "While the phenomenon of speaking in tongues, commonly associated with Pentecostalism, was not an experience sought or promoted by early Methodists, other equally startling manifestations of the Spirit did abound. This was particularly so as Methodism spread across the American frontier."[72] In the Pentecostal movement, it was also taught that, as a result of sanctification, believers would be endowed with the gifts of the Holy Spirit. It is interesting to note that many persons who became a part of the Pentecostal movement came out of the Methodist movement.

During this time of shifting theological paradigms as well as social change and upheaval, Seymour developed, and the Azusa Street Revival emerged. Seymour reluctantly answered his call to ministry while in Indianapolis. He later traveled to Houston, Texas, to search for family members. There he connected with the Houston Bible School, founded, and run by Charles Parham. During his years itinerating as a preacher, Parham founded various Bible schools that served as "healing and teaching missions."[73] Seymour attended Parham's Bible school in Houston to learn more about the Holy Spirit or the new Pentecost. Prior to establishing his Bible school in Houston, Parham had established Bible schools and missions in previous locations.

In Topeka, Kansas, at the Bethel Healing Home and Bethel Bible School, Parham cemented his understanding of the baptism of the Holy

---

[71]   Guidelines: The UMC and the Charismatic Movement, accessed May 24, 2017, http://www.umc.org/what-we-believe/guidelines-the-umc-and-the-charismatic-movement.

[72]   Guidelines: The UMC and the Charismatic Movement.

[73]   Robert R. Owens, *Speak to the Rock: The Azusa Street Revival.* (Lanham, MD: University Press of America. 1998), 49.

Spirit. Parham held as foundational to the faith the concept that speaking in tongues was the only evidence of reception of the baptism of the Holy Spirit. This foundational belief was bolstered by the completion of a class assignment he gave his students in Topeka, KS, while he was ministering away from the school. The assignment required students to scour the scriptures to determine evidence of the baptism of the Holy Spirit. The students determined that the only scriptural evidence of the baptism of the Holy Spirit was by glossolalia, speaking in tongues. In 1900, in response to the class revelation, one student, Agnes S. Ozman, asked for prayer and received the baptism of the Holy Spirit, as evidenced by speaking in an unlearned language. This revelation spread like wildfire.

While Seymour believed in racial harmony and equality, he lived in the dichotomy of his time. He studied at Parham's Bible school in Houston. While he studied and learned, he did not do so in the presence of his European American classmates. As an African American he was not allowed to sit in class with his white peers. In fact, he reportedly sat outside the classroom with the door cracked, so that he could hear the teachings and learn what he so passionately wanted to know about God and God's Spirit. While Parham taught Seymour, he reportedly had connections with or at least supported views of the KKK.[74] Parham later expressed disdain for the multiethnic makeup of the persons involved in the ministry on Azusa Street.

Nonetheless, Parham's teachings exerted substantial influence on the Azusa Street revival. His student, William J. Seymour, later left Houston to serve a ministry in Los Angeles, teaching the tenets of the faith learned in Topeka. Seymour had been invited to lead a ministry in Los Angeles. His teachings about speaking in tongues as a result of the baptism of the Holy Spirit were challenging and problematic to many of those he taught. As a result of the conflict, he was locked out of the church he had traveled to Los Angeles to serve.[75] As a consequence of the displacement from the

---

[74] J. Lee Grady, "Pentecostals Renounce Racism", December 12, 1994, accessed May 19, 2017, http://www.christianitytoday.com/ct/1994/december12/4te058. html; Cecil M. Robeck, Jr., "THE PAST: Historical Roots of Racial Unity and Division in American Pentecostalism," accessed May 19, 2017, http://www.pctii. org/cyberj/cyberj14/robeck.pdf, 9.

[75] Cecil M. Robeck, Jr., "THE PAST: Historical Roots of Racial Unity and Division in American Pentecostalism," accessed May 20, 2017, 13, http://www. pctii.org/cyberj/cyberj14/robeck.pdf.

church, he began teaching and leading prayer meetings at the home of a family who lived on Bonnie Brae Street. Interest in the ministry sparked after some in attendance began speaking in tongues. Many people heard what was happening and flocked to the ministry. The increase in persons present resulted in the need for a new meeting space. The new site for their growing ministry was 312 Azusa Street, Los Angeles, California. The ministry later became known as the Apostolic Faith Gospel Mission, taking its name from the ministry begun by Charles Parham. The revival that took place on Azusa Street impacted the entire world, as it spread the Pentecostal movement. Interestingly, Seymour didn't receive the baptism of the Holy Spirit until April 12, 1906, after he began teaching in Los Angeles.[76] The Azusa Street Revival began on April 9, 1906.

A Multiethnic New Pentecost Breaks Out at Azusa Street

From its inception, the Apostolic Faith Gospel Mission was a multiethnic community of believers. That reality, coupled with the ecstatic responses of the members, attracted tremendous attention in the community, reminiscent of the move of the Holy Spirit during the first Pentecost, after the resurrection of Jesus, detailed in Acts 2.

> When the day of Pentecost came, they were all together in one place.[2] suddenly a sound like the blowing of a violent wind came from heaven and filled the whole house where they were sitting. [3] They saw what seemed to be tongues of fire that separated and came to rest on each of them. [4] All of them were filled with the Holy Spirit and began to speak in other tongues[a] as the Spirit enabled them.[77]

Some individuals came in search of an authentic and powerful encounter with God. Others came to investigate that which didn't seem plausible. Individuals who flocked to the services were either seeking more from God or were just nosey about what was going on. The happenings at the Apostolic Faith Gospel Mission garnered attention from the area newspapers. According to an article in the *Los Angeles Times* on September 10, 1906,

---

[76] 312 Azusa.com, accessed May 20, 2017. https://312azusa.com/
[77] Acts 2: 1-4, New International Version, accessed May 27, 2017, Biblegateway.com.

All classes of people gathered in the temple last night. There were big negroes looking for a fight, there were little fairies dressed in dainty chiffon who stood on the benches and looked on with questioning wonder in their baby-blue eyes. There were cappers from North Alameda Street, and sedate dames from West Adams Street. There were all ages, sizes, colors, nationalities, and previous conditions of servitude.[78]

While the article wasn't particularly positive, it did broadcast the move of God on Azusa Street and resulted in others learning about and experiencing the ministry at the mission. It is interesting to note that there were reportedly numerous instances when the baptism of the Holy Spirit resulted in a person speaking in a language from another part of the world that he or she had not formally learned before.

The factors that contributed to the impact and influence of the Azusa Street revival appear to be complex; I suggest the following as the basic and perhaps most important reasons. They are:

1. The population growth in Los Angeles
2. The multiethnic reality of the city as evidenced by integration
3. The prayers of saints for a new outpouring of God's Holy Spirit
4. An initial openness to ignore racial and denominational differences as well as prescribed gender roles in order to benefit from what God was doing on Azusa Street.
5. A well developed and far-reaching communications process that reached thousands.[79]

During the time of this revival, Los Angeles was experiencing explosive growth. "Between 1880 and 1910 Los Angeles was the fastest growing city in the United States, the population doubled in the 1890s and tripled in

---

[78] "How Holy Roller Gets Religion." California Digital Newspaper Collection, *Los Angeles Herald*, Volume 33, Number 345, September 10, 1906, accessed May 20, 2017, https://cdnc.ucr.edu/cgibin/cdnc?a=d&d=LAH19060910.2.94.

[79] Robert R. Owens, *Speak to the Rock: The Azusa Street Revival*. (Lanham, MD: University Press of America, 1998), 54, 61. Larry Martin. *The Life and Ministry of William J. Seymour*. (Joplin, MO: Christian Life Books. 1999), 104-105, 119-127.

the first decade of the twentieth century."[80] The country was rife with the struggles of racism. However, "at the turn of the century, Los Angeles was better integrated than most American cities of the day."[81]

There appeared to be a desire to experience what the Holy Spirit was doing at the mission. Robert R. Owens identified the movement as demonstrating "a sociological aspect of anti-structural tendencies." The movement's openness to defying racial, gender, and denominational barriers was evidenced by the inter-racial and generally egalitarian nature of the meetings."[82] Owens reported that "Educated, uneducated, rich, poor, African Americans, Asians, Hispanics, whites, men, women, native born, recent immigrants and foreign visitors all prayed, sang, and came to the altar together."[83]

The ethnic and socio-economic diversity was attractive to many individuals. People from all over the world traveled to Azusa Street to experience the movement God was creating. Charles H. Mason, of the Church of God in Christ, and William Durham, father of the Assemblies of God Church, are just two who were touched by God's Pentecost through this ministry. Frank Bartleman, an eyewitness and minister himself, said this about the movement: "At Azusa Street, the color line was washed away in the Blood."[84]

This experience of God's multiethnic revival at Azusa Street was powerful yet short-lived. For the duration of the revival—three years—prayer was nonstop, and services were held constantly. "Azusa Street lasted three and a half years. Every night and every day, it never ceased. There was always a service or someone seeking the baptism of the Holy Spirit with the evidence of the speaking of tongues continuously for three and half years

---

80   Owens, *Speak to the Rock: The Azusa Street Revival*, 54, 61. Martin. *The Life and Ministry of William J. Seymour*, 54.

81   Owens, *Speak to the Rock: The Azusa Street Revival*, 55.

82   Robert R. Owens, *Speak to the Rock: The Azusa Street Revival*. (Lanham, MD: University Press of America, 1998), 67.

83   Owens, *Speak to the Rock: The Azusa Street Revival*, 67.

84   Vinson Synan, "Pentecostalism: William Seymour, Issue 65: Ten Influential Christians of the 20st Century," Christianity Today.com, accessed May 9, 2017, http://www.christianitytoday.com/history/issues/issue65/pentecostalism-william-seymour.html.

non-stop.[85] The Azusa Street Mission was known as a place where people were healed. Reportedly, crutches of healed individuals were placed on the walls of the mission as a testimony of God's healing power at Azusa Street.

In 1974, Azusa Street researcher Vinson Synan interviewed the only known survivors at that time: the Rev. Lawrence Katly or (Catlett,) at the Church of God in Christ in Pasadena, CA, and Ms. Mattie Cummings. Both attended the mission as children, experienced healings, and recounted their memories of the revival. As a child Ms. Mattie (or Maddie) was deaf and unable to attend school. At the services, she received prayer and gained her hearing. Rev. Katly suffered from tuberculosis (TB). He was delivered from TB; a reality that he said was confirmed by lung specialists during World War Two.[86]

Ms. Mattie shared what was taught at the mission. They were taught, "You must first be converted, you must be sanctified, and God would fill you with a sanctified life through his precious Holy Spirit and you would speak in tongues as the evidence."[87] Rev. Katly added his observations and experiences. "Every gift that was listed in the scriptures was practiced in the Azusa Mission."[88] Both commented on the way people of various colors coexisted at the Azusa Street Mission. Ms. Mattie said, "One thing that was so nice, nobody ever said 'you are black' or 'you are white,' but we were just children of God praising and rejoicing in God. We were all praising God."[89]

An effective communications strategy enhanced the mission's outreach, contact, and growth. The mission newspaper, *The Apostolic Faith*, enjoyed a substantial circulation. Started in September 1906, the publication "grew to twenty thousand subscribers within a few months…a number which more than doubled by the following year."[90] The subscription list grew as

---

85   Roberts Liardon, "God's Generals," accessed May 27, 2017, http://godsgenerals. com/generals-video/.

86   Katly, Lawrence and Mattie Cummings. Interview with Vinson Synan. I've been unable to confirm the correct spelling of the Azusa Mission eyewitnesses. Accessed May 29, 2017. https://www.youtube.com/watch?v=THOCgQqWKFo.

87   Katly, Lawrence and Mattie Cummings. Interview with Vinson Synan.

88   Katly, Lawrence and Mattie Cummings. Interview with Vinson Synan.

89   Katly, Lawrence and Mattie Cummings. Interview with Vinson Synan.

90   Roberts Liardon, "God's Generals: William J. Seymour," accessed May 27, 2017, http://godsgenerals.com/williamseymour/.

large as 50,000 people. This was long before email, twitter, and Facebook. The ability to connect with people all over the world was greatly enhanced by the newspaper. The circulars included testimonials of people whose lives were touched by God in the mission, as well as sermons and other teachings by Seymour.

That said, the movement was by no means without critics. People who attended services and prayer meetings gave witness of numerous conversions, healings, and incidents when people spoke in other unlearned tongues or languages, known or unknown. Leary of the new movement, numerous religious leaders dissuaded their members from attending and even spoke disparagingly about the Azusa Street Mission Revival. Some saw this new movement as a cult or, worse, even satanic. Much of the mainstream media's portrayal of the movement was negative. Various entities, including the Health and Fire Departments attempted to shut the ministry down.[91]

The Revival came to end three and a half years after its inception, for the following reasons:

- Racism and the cultural mores of the times
- Doubt related to the authenticity of the move of the Holy Spirit at Azusa Street
- Communication efforts intentionally thwarted from internal sources
- Jealousy[92]

While the movement was countercultural in its multiethnic approach, its socioeconomic interactions, and in the way it viewed gender roles, the dominant culture was nevertheless present and exercised significant influence on the ministry. Culture demanded compliance to the mores of the time. Racism, whether overt or subconscious, made itself known even among people in this movement. This was the case even among leaders in the new move of Pentecostalism. Charles Parham, Seymour's former teacher, and the person who had ordained Seymour as a minister, expressed disdain towards the worship services at the Azusa Street Mission.

---

[91]   Robert R. Owens, *Speak to the Rock: The Azusa Street Revival*. (Lanham, MD: University Press of America. 1998), 65.

[92]   Owens, *Speak to the Rock: The Azusa Street Revival*, 88-89, 105.

Parham thought the people were too emotional. Additionally, he expressed concern about the mingling of the races. In a recount of what he observed in the Mission's Upper Room, he shared, "...men and women, whites and blacks, knelt together or fell across one another."[93] For some, the close proximity of people of various races, cultures and ethnicities was a challenge and resulted in racist responses. External and internal forces worked to cause the ministry to split along color lines. Leadership of the Azusa Street Mission, possibly in response to racism, decided that the Mission was open to all, yet to be led by only African American leadership.

Seymour's marriage also caused a rift. Seymour married Jenny Evans Moore Seymour, an African American woman. Clara Lum and Florence Crawford, both of European American ancestry, opposed the marriage. Some argue that the women thought Rev. Seymour should not have married at all due to the imminent return of Jesus. Another explanation offered was that Florence Crawford had romantic feelings for Rev. Seymour and wanted to marry him herself. It is reported that C.H. Mason discouraged Crawford from marrying Seymour because it wasn't time to marry across color lines. [94] Whatever the explanation, the two women took the newspaper mailing list in anger, and left California for Portland, Oregon. As a result, Seymour and the Azusa Street Mission were unable to communicate with the thousands of people on the subscription list. This setback ultimately proved fatal to the movement.

What Congregations Can Learn from the Azusa Street Revival

The revival on Azusa Street provides keen and invaluable insight to multiethnic ministry in general, and to numerous churches.

- The people were united in their mission and desire for more of what the Holy Spirit was doing.

---

93 Larry Martin, *The Life and Ministry of William J. Seymour* (Joplin, MO: Christian Life Books, 1999), 269.

94 Larry Martin, *The Life and Ministry of William J. Seymour* (Joplin, MO: Christian Life Books, 1999), 76; Vinson Synan, "Pentecostalism: William Seymour," *Christianity Today*, Issue 65, accessed June 1, 2017, http://www.christianitytoday.com/history/issues/issue65/pentecostalism-william-seymour.html.

- Individuals engaged in the revival were involved in spiritual disciplines. Prayer and worship were on-going at the Azusa Street Mission Revival
- As evidenced by the Azusa Street Mission Revival, a ministry can impact its immediate community and world.
- The ministry adhered to a life where all were equal—despite culture, gender, and socio-economic reality.
- The revival valued personal interactions and stood against the "-isms" that will attempt to creep into the Christian community and stop the move of God.

Those who became a part of the Azusa Street movement were yearning for more from God, wanting people to receive a touch from the Holy Spirit and to tell others about Jesus. There is no limit to what can and will happen when people of faith join together to seek and worship God and to spread the news of God's goodness to everyone. It is not my assertion that every member of the church must speak in tongues. Rather, it is my heart's desire that everyone present experience what God is doing now, as evidenced by the move of the Holy Spirit. Every congregation has the call to carry its community in its heart. When the congregation—of one accord with each other and the Holy Spirit—lives out its mission, things will begin to happen in its neighborhood, zip code, and beyond.

It is vitally important for the congregational ministry leadership to reflect the diversity of the community. The experience of the Azusa Street Revival is invaluable to our current reality. It took place during a time of extreme racial segregation and racism. We find ourselves in a time of racial polarization.

Today, America is again at a racial crossroads. On one hand, our country and communities exhibit multicultural and multiethnic sensitivity. On the other hand, racial intolerance appears to be on the rise. Weekly, if not daily, news stories about racism or racial injustice abound. The multiethnic bridge-building experience of the Azusa Street Revival is invaluable to congregations of our day.

Multiethnic bridge-building is especially important for congregations that strive to connect with and engage in ministry in our increasingly racially and culturally diverse communities. God has positioned each congregation to share the good news of Jesus Christ with its neighbors. Numerous congregations provide meeting space for community organizations. God desires those churches who provide a ministry of hospitality for community meetings to engage with the individuals who come across the church threshold.

Quite often there exists a disconnect between congregations and the neighborhoods in which they are located. As congregations age, they often become more internally focused and end up placing more attention on self-preservation and maintenance of the building, then spreading the good news to and cultivating relationship with neighbors. That was the case for Cheverly United Methodist Church, CUMC, where I currently serve as pastor. In a community with a predominant population of African Americans, this congregation is still predominantly European American. When my Doctor of Ministry Project was first implemented, from which this book was derived, the congregation had significant numbers of cultures present—Asian, Asian Indian, African, Hispanic, African American, and European American. Even so, CUMC battles perceptions that it is a "white church." Even people who have lived in the community for years think the congregation has a white membership. A question the congregation had to ask itself is "How can it reach its diverse community of neighbors?

The following exchange with a neighbor demonstrates community perceptions about CUMC. Every year the Tabitha Circle of the United Methodist Women used to purchase food for the creation of ten substantial Easter food boxes/baskets for the children at Gladys Noon Spellman Elementary School. The baskets are distributed prior to the Christmas and Easter breaks to ensure that children and their families have enough food to eat during the holiday. Two-thirds of the school population is eligible for free or reduced lunches. To increase the numbers of families that could be served, church and community members were asked to donate food or money for the creation of the food baskets. One community member, an African American woman who had lived in the community for more than ten years, donated food for the effort. Although she knew about the church she had never been in it. Additionally, she shared that she thought that CUMC was a white church. She was surprised that the pastor was African American. I'm the fourth pastor of color, and third African American pastor to serve the congregation.

This woman was not alone. One afternoon while walking the neighborhood, two laity and I visited neighbors to discern three things:

1. What do you know about Cheverly United Methodist Church?
2. What are some of the needs of the community?
3. What can Cheverly United Methodist Church do to address those needs?

Most individuals who lived on the street behind the church had never attended and knew nothing about the church. One woman's older daughter had attended the church-sponsored Weekday Nursery, yet she knew nothing about the church's ministry. Her younger child was preparing to attend Weekday Nursery in the fall. Every congregation would benefit from canvassing the community to learn what the community knows about the church and discern the expressed needs of the neighborhood.

The Opportunity to Engage the Entire Community Awaits

According to a LifeWay Research survey released in January of 2015, "Sunday morning remains one of the most segregated hours in American life, with more than 8 in 10 congregations made up of one predominant racial group.[95] Interestingly, the research indicates that 53% of respondents do not believe their church needs to become more ethnically diverse, while 40% believe they do need to be more ethnically diverse, and 7% are not sure.[96] In communities where racial diversity is nonexistent, these findings would make sense, but this research is challenging to any community. This nation is increasingly multiethnic. Congregations now have the opportunity, led by the Holy Spirit, to break through barriers of race, gender, and cultural/ethnic differences to minister more fully in a diverse community.

It is my belief that disciple-making in many congregations has diminished, which was caused by and resulted in a loss of understanding of the mission of the church and a low prioritization for reaching new people

---

[95] Bob Smetlana, "Sunday Morning in America is Still Segregated-And That's Ok With Worshipers," LifeWay Research, 2014, accessed May 11, 2017, http://lifeway research.com/2015/01/15/sunday-morning-in-america-still-segregated-and-thats-ok-with-worshipers/.

[96] Smetlana, "Sunday Morning in America is Still Segregated-And That's Ok With Worshipers."

for Christ, even the numerous people in the surrounding neighborhoods. Congregations would benefit from the creation or strengthening of an intentional disciple-making system. As Christ followers within the church are discipled, they themselves are enlisted to disciple others. Disciples make disciples. Strengthening the disciple-making system will strengthen the congregation's Kingdom-building and help the church connect with neighbors. Congregants can connect with community members and facilitate the development of relationships and ministry to and with the community. Bridge-building is especially necessary so that the congregation can more effectively reach neighbors in their socio-economically, ethnically, racially, and culturally diverse community, with the transforming love of Jesus Christ and through the power of the Holy Ghost.

FOUR

Theological Foundations

Theology Informs Action

WHO IS GOD? IS THERE a God? What relationship does humanity have with God? What purpose does God have for humans or the world? These are just a few questions humans struggle with each day. Everyone is a theologian, engaging theology, in one way or another. Atheists and agnostics engage theology, even if disparagingly. The definition of theology is: "the study of God and of religious doctrines and matters of divinity."[97]

A person's theology is demonstrated or communicated through his or her beliefs, words, and actions. The way a person lives and engages in community with others gives witness to his or her theological stance. What theological beliefs are held by Christians for whom the ways of the faith have grown cold? I contend that we live in a time when many in the Christian community of faith struggle with spiritual amnesia. Paul Nixon explains that spiritual amnesia "... is spiritual life divorced from Christian memory and awkwardly connected, if at all, with the historic Christian mission."[98] This spiritual amnesia pervades our contemporary reality, just as it did during time periods leading up to previous revivals. The disciplines of corporate bible study and prayer meetings are exercised by just a few. Today in many congregations, evangelism, or faith-sharing,

---

[97] Michael Agnes, editor, *Webster's New World Compact Desk Dictionary*. (Cleveland, OH: Wiley Publishing, Inc. 2002), 499-500.

[98] Paul Nixon, *Healing Spiritual Amnesia: Remembering What it Means to Be the Church*. (Nashville, TN: Abingdon Press, 2004), 19.

carries as much stigma as the proverbial four-letter word. Many Christ followers, when asked, admit to anxiety or unease about praying in public.

While many Christian congregations serve their communities through social services and concern themselves with securing the future of their buildings, those efforts are not the main missions of people of faith. Spiritual amnesia has resulted in ministry devoid of the original mission of the church—discipling believers who will disciple others. Further, spiritual amnesia affects or is formed by one's theology. I offer the following observation about the state of many Christian congregations:

- Hospitality extended toward community members and organizations instead of and/or devoid of evangelism/faith sharing
- Attending to the work of the church rather than attending to ministry unto the Lord
- Maintaining and addressing the needs of those already in congregations versus inviting non-church members to join them in their faith journey with Christ
- Maintenance of the status quo instead of "social disruption"[99]
- An inward ministry focus instead of an externally focused ministry and outreach approach
- Homogeneous ministry versus multi-ethnic, multi-cultural and diverse ministry
- Discipleship in many established congregations is a challenged reality
- Evangelism is avoided because of the belief that all religions are equal, and the belief that Jesus is not really needed because all paths lead to God
- The notion of evangelism is offensive to many within the church
- The delivery of social services is devoid of the good news
- Fellowship with others at church supersedes personal fellowship with God
- Shunning the power of the Holy Spirit and choosing human power instead

---

[99] The term social disruption was shared by Marlon Hall in his presentation "Faith and Innovation," delivered at the Immerse Conference: Where Spirituality and Innovation Connect," St. John's Downtown UMC, Houston, TX, March 17, 2017.

In many congregations, disciple-making has diminished, which has resulted in and/or was caused by a loss of understanding of the mission of the church and a low priority for reaching new people for Christ. A recovery of missional understanding will result in a congregation of stronger disciples, who will engage and reach out to others in the pews and beyond the church walls with the good news of God's kingdom love. How can one share a faith that he or she cannot articulate? A reclamation of mission is made possible when Christ followers and congregations revisit theological roots.

There exist many who would disagree with my contention. Those individuals could contend that the mission of the church has changed since the early days of the Christian Church. Early Christ followers were enlisted to share the good news of God's kingdom with others. Now, the Christian mission is serving others through social services. Additionally, it could be said that because many religions exist, it is no longer appropriate to push Christianity on anyone else. There must be more than one way to God. Christ can't possibly be the only way. A portion of the church believes that the Holy Spirit has ceased functioning as the Holy Spirit operated during the first Pentecost after Jesus' resurrection or during the various revivals throughout history. Others believe that the power that God once demonstrated through the Holy Spirit no longer seems to exist. Therefore, the church has no power. If that assumption is true, the predominant mode of ministry in mainline denominations (despite the fact that it is resulting in consistent decline of disciples and worship attendance) must be correct.

In the following pages of this chapter, the following theological themes will be addressed:

- God's Call to Community
- Community of believers
- The Mission of God – Salvation available for all

This chapter will engage practical theology, as lived out through the Azusa Street Revival, with attention to missiology as the modes of study. Practical theology deals with how a believer lives out his or her faith. Practical theology focuses on how people embody their faith. "Practical theology focuses on human praxis as a point of departure and the mutual interlocutory relationship between practices and theory and their sources."[100] Specifically, this paper will interface with missiology, which in itself is part of the practical theology umbrella.

It is my contention that this chapter will demonstrate the existence of a direct correlation between our theology and the praxis of our faith. Praxis, the practice of our faith, is reflective of our theology – our understanding of who God is and who we are in relationship to God. Praxis directly affects church vitality. This chapter will undergird this book theologically by showing how the personal discipleship of congregational leaders and the congregation's discipleship system, empowered by the Holy Spirit, will result in a reclamation of the mission of the church and increase the church's priority of reaching new people for Jesus Christ.

Theology Influences Mission

What is missiology and how does it inform our theological enterprise? Missiology is defined as "the theological study of mission of the church, especially the character and purpose of missionary work."[101] Missiologist, Ed Stetzer, explains: "Missiology is accomplished at the intersection of gospel, culture, and the church. It is a multi-disciplinary study that incorporates theology, anthropology/sociology, and ecclesiology."[102] Stetzer adds that "Missiology is not only grounded in theological reflection, it is also grounded in anthropological/ sociological research. Missiology requires thoughtful engagement with the human situation in light of theology and the task of Christian mission."[103]

Current Christian practice, in many instances, appears strikingly distinct from those of the early Christian church. Worship attendance, while not weekly for many people, remains regular. For many congregations, infrequent worship is the order of the day. It is the new or next normal.

---

[100] Dale P. Andrews and Robert London Smith, Jr., editors, *Black Practical Theology*, (Waco,TX: Baylor University Press, 2015), 4.

[101] Dictionary.com, http://www.dictionary.com/browse/missiology. Accessed November 26, 2017.

[102] Ed Stetser, "What is a Missiologist? The Theology, Tools, and a Team of a Missiologist. June 10, 2013. CT (Christianity Today), accessed on November 26, 2017. https://www.christianitytoday.com/edstetzer/2013/june/what-is-missiologist.html.

[103] Stetser, "What is a Missiologist? The Theology, Tools, and a Team of a Missiologist.

The COVID-19 pandemic has further complicated things as worship engagement is now through on-line worship, parking lot worship, worship in the sanctuary or a hybrid model. The historical emphasis shared earlier, the Azusa Street Revival, shared numerous similarities with the early Christian Church as recounted in the Acts of the Apostles. Our current context appears markedly different from both Azusa Street and the Acts of the Apostles. In both latter settings, the Holy Spirit's power was present and actively evident in the lives of people of all colors, cultures, socio-economic realities, and genders. In Acts 10: 44-45, the Holy Spirit moved upon people from all walks of life, including Jewish and Gentile Christian believers:

> While Peter was still speaking these words, the Holy Spirit came on all who heard the message. The circumcised believers who had come with Peter were astonished that the gift of the Holy Spirit had been poured out even on Gentiles.[104] Acts 10: 44-45 NIV

This reality is notable because God broke religious and societal barriers between Jewish and Gentile Christian believers. To the amazement of a society wracked with racism and sexism, the Holy Spirit moved again to bridge socio-economic, racial, cultural, denominational, and gender divides during the Azusa Street Revival. Through these examples, God defies the world system to create a multi-cultural and economically diverse community of believers. The Azusa Street Revival and the Pentecostal community in Acts 10: 44-48 and Isaiah 56: 1-8 are similar in that God shattered societal barriers while calling believers into an intimate relationship with Jesus Christ.

Inherent in the Azusa Street Revival and reflective of the entire Acts of the Apostles, as well as the Isaiah 56 passage, is an emphasis placed upon believers to live out a personal ministry. During the Azusa Street Revival everyone was expected and invited to actively live out their faith. Each person, lay and ordained, fulfilled ministry as part of the priesthood of all believers. These examples give witness to the priesthood of all believers.

> There was an essence to the Pentecostal Revival from the beginning that compelled everyone to not to just learn about the Lord, but to know Him through personal

---

[104] Acts 10: 44-45, NIV Bible Gateway, accessed on November 26, 2017, https://www.biblegateway.com/passage/?search=Acts%2010:44-45.

experience. People were taught not just to be spectators, but to demonstrate.[105]

In today's contemporary mainline congregations, spectatorship often seems the predominant mode of ministry. Demonstration is assigned to the clergy. Clergy, by default, have earned the role of being the prayers, the Bible students/scholars, evangelists, and connectors with individuals outside of the church walls. If demonstration was an expected part of life and ministry of people of the early church or the Azusa Street Revival, what are the implications for today's Christian believers? Demonstration is indicative of praxis. Praxis is indicative of theology. For the purpose of this chapter, demonstration is defined as "the action or process of showing the existence or truth of something by giving proof or evidence."[106] Joseph E. Bush, Jr. explains, "Praxis is the Greek word meaning 'practice.' In contemporary theology and educational theory, praxis refers to the process of reflection itself, which attends to practice. It refers to any method that allows us to reflect critically or analytically on practice."[107] The current state of praxis or demonstration by many Christ followers communicates a theology markedly different from the early church and the Azusa Street Revival. What theological understanding underlies this reality? Our theological understanding of mission, or our missiology, greatly impacts our praxis.

Theology impacts how we live and is influenced by our beliefs. Doing theology does not require a religious degree. We do theology in our everyday lives. "We are doing theology when we pray, worship, read Scripture, teach others about the faith and make decisions about how to live in right relationship with God."[108] Additionally, we are doing theology when we make decisions about how to be in right relationship to others. "The traditional goal of Christian theology is to develop a better understanding of God so that we can think and speak rightly about God within the

---

[105]   Rick Joyner, *The Power to Change the World: The Welsh and Azusa Street Revivals*, (Fort Mill, SC: Morning Star Publications, Inc. 2006), 53.

[106]   Encycopedia.com, accessed on November 8, 2017, http://www.encyclopedia. com/social-sciences-and-law/law/law/demonstration.

[107]   Joseph E Bush, Jr. *Practical Theology in Church and Society*. (Eugene, OR: Cascade Books. 2016), 5.

[108]   Keith L. Johnson. Theology as Discipleship. (Downers Grove, IL: IVP Academic, 2015), 18.

context of a life governed by our faith in Christ and our discipleship to him in community with other Christians."[109] Individuals and their actions are shaped by the actions of their congregations. If a low missiology exists within the congregation, individual and corporate praxis reflects that reality by a discipleship in which observance of the spiritual disciplines has been abandoned and personal mission and evangelism have been forgotten. "One of the central tasks of practical theology is to consider the relationship between how the Church and individual Christians have considered the meaning of faith in light of what individuals and the Church actually do in their daily lived attempts to give expression to what they believe."[110]

God's Call to Community

Made by God to reflect God's image in the world, humanity often flees the presence and guidance of its Creator. We humans are peculiar. While we yearn meaning that only truly comes from our relationship with God, we often abandon the "Lover of our Souls." Each day of our existence we remain beloved by God, even when we deny or ignore our Creator. Through it all, God desires to be in relationship with humanity. Why wouldn't God limit Godself to a heavenly or other realm apart from human interaction? Why would God want to deal with humans? God desires community with humanity. God fellowshipped with humanity in the Garden of Eden. Even when Adam and Eve broke relationship with the Divine, God's nature of love continued towards them. God's very nature is love. God's love is made known to humanity continually as demonstrated in the Hebrew and Christian Scriptures. God created Adam and Eve to be in community with God. God initiated relationship with Abram and Sarai, a childless couple in old age, and later made them the matriarch and patriarch of countless generations and nations. God later freed their descendants who had become an enslaved people in Egypt. Through relationship with God, formerly enslaved Hebrew people were marked by God's divine identification of favor and connection with God. It was these

---

[109] Johnson. Theology as Discipleship, 34.

[110] Anthony G. Reddie. *Is God Colour-blind? Insights from Black Theology for Christian Ministry*. (London, England: Society for Promoting Christian Knowledge, 2009), xiii.

individuals who gave witness to God's power, grace, and love to others. Through countless generations, God has demonstrated and continues to show a love for all people, even those who have been marginalized by society, or stigmatized with the identifiable "isms" of racism, sexism, etc.

God seeks community with humans due to God's divine love. God continuously woos humanity, inviting each person to lovingly respond to God's advances so that God can conduct, what the Rev. Dr. Rudy Rasmus calls, "a love takeover," to expand God's kingdom on earth. God works through God's community of believers to work God's plan of redemption and restoration, peace, and provision.

Throughout the ages, people have disagreed about who is and who is not a legitimate or desired member of God's community. In Jewish thought, faithful eunuchs and Gentiles were considered unwanted and were therefore unwelcome in the temple by faithful Jewish believers. Eunuchs and some Gentile ethnic groups were expressly excluded from the Jewish Assembly by the Law of Moses. "No one who has been emasculated by crushing or cutting may enter the assembly of the LORD."[111] Deuteronomy 23: 1, NIV

It would be a challenge for faithful Jews to imagine that people previously excluded had obtained a welcome in God's assembly. The Isaiah text gives witness to that contention. "Let no foreigner who is bound to the LORD say, 'The LORD will surely exclude me from his people.' And let no eunuch complain, 'I am only a dry tree.'"[112] Isaiah 56:3, NIV

The recipients of this text were blessed by God and enjoyed a special place of favor with God. They were blessed to eventually be a blessing to the entire world. This Isaiah text joined other passages through which God reminded the entire world of God's plan to offer salvation to people of all nations.

> It is too small a thing for you to be my servant to restore the tribes of Jacob and bring back those of Israel I have kept. I will also make you a light for the Gentiles, that my salvation may reach to the ends of the earth.[113] Isaiah 49:6, NIV

---

[111] Deuteronomy 23:1, NIV, accessed on August 19, 2022, https://www.biblegateway.com/passage/?search=Deuteronomy+23%3A+1&version=NIV.

[112] Isaiah 56:3, NIV, accessed on November 25, 2017, https://www.biblegateway.com/passage/?search=Isaiah%2056:1-8.

[113] Isaiah 49:6, NIV, accessed on November 27, 2017, https://www.biblegateway.com/passage/?search=Isaiah+49&version=NIV.

In the Isaiah 56 text, God informs those already set aside for God, the Hebrews, that God desires others to join the Divine community.

For this is what the LORD says:

> 'To the eunuchs who keep my Sabbaths,
> who choose what pleases me
> and hold fast to my covenant—
> [5] to them I will give within my temple and its walls
> a memorial and a name
> better than sons and daughters;
> I will give them an everlasting name
> that will endure forever.
> [6] And foreigners who bind themselves to the LORD
> to minister to him,
> to love the name of the LORD,
> and to be his servants,
> all who keep the Sabbath without desecrating it
> and who hold fast to my covenant—[114]
> [7] these I will bring to my holy mountain
> and give them joy in my house of prayer.' Isaiah 56: 4-7, NIV

In the Acts 10: 44-48 passage God again embraces Gentiles. To the surprise of faithful Jewish Christians, the Holy Spirit embraces Gentiles with God's favor.

> [44] While Peter was still speaking these words, the Holy Spirit came on all who heard the message. [45] The circumcised believers who had come with Peter were astonished that the gift of the Holy Spirit had been poured out even on Gentiles. [46] For they heard them speaking in tongues and praising God. Then Peter said, [47] "Surely no one can stand in the way of their being baptized with water. They have received the Holy Spirit just as we have." [48] So he ordered that they be baptized in the name of Jesus Christ.[115] Acts 10: 44-48, NIV

---

[114] Isaiah 56:4-7, NIV, accessed on November 25, 2017. https://www.biblegateway.com/passage/?search=Isaiah%2056:1-8.

[115] Acts 10:44-48, NIV, accessed on November 25, 2017, https://www.biblegateway.com/passage/?search=Acts+10%3A+44-48&version=NIV.

Through both scriptures God enlarges the circle of God's beloved community of faith. The concept of a prescribed and biblical homogeneity is thus challenged, and divine diversity becomes a divine desired norm. Equipped with the understanding of God's mission, God's followers were invited to take God's lead in mission and ministry with the "other."

Belief drives and directs praxis. If the community of believers adheres to the belief that some people, because of culture, ethnicity, gender, or socio-economic standing, are "less than," cursed, or forsaken, most likely the other is not welcome into the worshipping community of believers. Exclusion of the unwanted "other" would be the spoken or unspoken rule of the house of worship. The person deemed "other" would be shown disdain and disrespect. In cases where individuals deemed "other" are allowed into the community of faith, they are often prescribed an inferior status—segregated seating, limitations in leadership roles, etc.

To this day, a conversation continues about who can be in community with God, who can be saved, and who is not worthy of salvation. Christian worship in the United States is still highly segregated. That reality points to a theological belief, held by the many of the most powerful in society, that God favors their privilege over the plight of the oppressed. Countering previous and contemporary claims of the homogeneity of God's love, God demonstrates the truth and reality that divine love extends to all. The barriers of socio-economic differences, gender, color, ethnicity, culture, and denominational affiliation melt in God's presence. The Holy Spirit is not confined by the human sin of prejudice related to any "isms." God is a God of the oppressed, not just the oppressors. Any individual who seeks relationship with God is deemed welcome. God's actions of divine love for all wreaks havoc on congregations and Christ followers who refuse to engage and welcome their culturally diverse neighbors.

In the family of God, our lives are interrelated. I am because you are. In this instance, the African understanding of "Ubuntu" provides a challenge to Christians to live in community despite society's -isms. We are connected. All lives are interwoven and valued. This truth is all the more understood because we are part of the Christian community of faith. "A Zulu and Xhosa word that means 'community,'…its rich meaning is perhaps best captured in the Zulu saying, umntu, ngumntu, ngbantu, which means, 'an individual can only be fully human by being in relationship with other human beings, all of whom have their humanity validated by virtue of the ntu (the breath of God!) within them.'"[116]

Both biblical passages, as well as the move of the Holy Spirit during the Azusa Street Revival, demonstrated a Divine commitment to multi-cultural, multi-ethnic ministry. Just as God initiated connection with people beyond previously established societal barriers, so we, as members of God's community, are called to do likewise.

God's community of believers is called to live in right relationship with God and others. When Christians practice racism, sexism, socio-economic prejudice, or even intentional exclusion of disenfranchised or marginalized people, what do their actions communicate theologically about God? Does that behavior give witness to the belief that God is anti-woman, anti-people of color, anti-poor, etc.? If praxis communicates theology, what does racism practiced by Christians communicate theologically about their understanding about God? How can mistreatment of any human being based on color, economics, gender, or physical deformity by Christians be applauded or deemed acceptable by people of faith? Is the cause of this behavior misinformation, the absence of theological understanding, or malevolence among Christians? Is it spiritual amnesia or evil intent? Is it possible that Christian congregations and Christ-followers have forgotten the importance of loving what God loves? God loves all people. Practical theology and missiology may prove helpful in teaching people more about God's heart, hopefully resulting in human change.

It is interesting to note that numerous congregations are situated in multi-ethnic and multi-cultural communities, yet intentionally remain homogenous. For some congregations, the cause may be rooted in fear. In other congregations, the reason for not seeking community with the "other" may be an inability to see in persons of different cultures, ethnicities, socio-economic or linguistic groups, the very image of God. The sins of "isms" blocks our ministry in intentional diverse community. Racism is a major hindrance to people's ability to see the image of God in people different from themselves.

---

[116] Jeremiah A. Wright Jr. "Doing Theology for Ordinary Folk," *Black Practical Theology*, ed. Dale P. Andrews and Robert London Smith Jr. (Waco, TX: Baylor University Press, 2015), 91.

Willie James Jennings contends that we, in the West, struggle with the aesthetic of whiteness. "We have yielded our collective imaginations to white aesthetic supremacy, signaling with every turn of media currents its right of way."[117] If, in our Western Christian understanding, our collective understanding assigns beauty, status, or worth to people based on an aesthetic of whiteness, which I would add often includes affluence, then consciously or unconsciously individuals of other hues, ethnicities, cultures, pigments, abilities, or socio-economic realities are deemed inferior, and therefore can be unwanted in many congregations. How can a person see God in him or herself if that person feels that he/she does not reflect the image of the Western dominant society? How can a person see God in another if that person does not reflect the expected or acceptable aesthetic of whiteness, beauty, or status? Jennings suggests that the path of liberation from this faulty aesthetic requires the creation of an "artistic ecclesiology,"[118] as well as the "cultivation of a creative critique of the prevailing racial aesthetic."[119]

The question can be raised, 'are churches ready and willing to live in God's divine community'? Time will tell. For too many congregations, the answer is still no. "Many churches are not yet ready to live in the real intimacy of human life constituted by the body of Jesus. They have not yet grasped that God has become flesh and has now opened our flesh to life eternal in community."[120]

True Christian community is not possible in the presence of hatred or other "isms" because true community is comprised of people who reflect the diversity found in God's creation. This was the case in the early church, and it is true today. Christian community includes people who are marginalized by society as was the case in the early church. In the faith community all were welcome– the poor, racial ethnics, tax collectors, and

---

[117] Willie James Jennings. "The Aesthetic Struggle and Ecclesial Vision," in *Black Practical Theology*, ed. Dale P. Andrews and Robert London Smith, Jr. (Waco, TX: Baylor University Press, 2015), 172.

[118] Jennings, "The Aesthetic Struggle and Ecclesial Vision," in *Black Practical Theology*, 182.

[119] Jennings, "The Aesthetic Struggle and Ecclesial Vision," in *Black Practical Theology*, 184.

[120] Jennings. "The Aesthetic Struggle and Ecclesial Vision," in *Black Practical Theology*, 185.

slaves. Membership in the household of faith is not contingent upon merit, but God's unmerited favor.

> There was room in the early Church for simple fisherman from Galilee, for erstwhile Zealots such as Simon and one-time tax-collectors of whom Matthew was typical, for the likes of Paul, an erudite Pharisee, for members of the nobility such as Manaen who grew up with Herod, for Jews and Greeks, for blacks from Africa, among them the eunuch from Ethiopia and Simon caller Niger who served with Paul as an elder in Antioch, for the slave Onesimus but also for his master Philemon, for prisoners no less than members of the imperial guard, and for a captain in the Roman army.[121]

In the current milieu, the aesthetic of whiteness stands in the way of true Divine community. Jennings invites us to consider the alternate to the aesthetic of whiteness. "That alternative aesthetic born of the Holy Spirit brings peoples together in shared desire, appreciation, and celebration of one another."[122] The Holy Spirit brought together Jew and Gentile in the Isaiah and Acts of the Apostles texts. It was the Holy Spirit who brought together those inside and outside society's margins—the eunuch, foreigners, and Hebrews as evidenced by the Isaiah 56 passage. The Holy Spirit brought together people of various ethnicities, including descendants of former slaves and former slave owners in the Azusa Street Revival.

As this paper was first being written, the United States found itself reeling from rising racial discord and increased activity of white nationalists and supremacists. In August 2017, this reality reached a boiling point as a Unite the Right rally in Charlottesville, VA was met with counter protestors. The result was the death of counter protestor Heather Heyer and the injuries of twenty other anti-racism protestors hit by a car driven by James Alex Fields.

This increase of racial hostility in the United States attracted the world's attention. The United Nations issued a warning to the US calling for the

---

[121] David J. Bosch, *Witness to the World*. (Atlanta, GA: John Knox Press, 1980), 223.

[122] Willie James Jennings, "The Aesthetic Struggle and Ecclesial Vision," in *Black Practical Theology*, ed. Dale P. Andrews and Robert London Smith, Jr. (Waco, TX: Baylor University Press, 2015), 185.

condemnation of racist crimes and speech.[123] Non-European descended foreigners, especially Latino or Africana, appear to be personas non-grata as evidenced by the rescinding of the Deferred Action for Childhood Arrivals and Temporary Protected Status for Nicaraguans and Haitians. Racism continues to rear its ugly head in the United States as evidenced by the shooting of African Americans attending a prayer meeting at Mother Emmanuel African Methodist Church, a crime committed by a European American raised in a Christian church. Where is God's church and what is God's church communicating theologically about the nature and presence of God?

Throughout history, God has blessed God's Community of Believers so that they can be a blessing to others. God has chosen men, women, and communities of believers to fulfill God's kingdom purpose on the earth. The blessing is not solely for the benefit of the recipient. "…a few are chosen to be the bearers of the purpose; they are chosen, not for themselves, but for the sake of all."[124] God's blessing and favor are to be shared.

Every congregation is a bearer of God's blessing that invites people into reconciled relationship with God. Yet, when Christians and congregations forget their God ordained mission, then the blessing bearers forgo some of their assignment. In the presence of missional amnesia, ministry praxis suffers.

The Mission of God

Throughout the Hebrew and Christian Scriptures, God has expressly sought people to share community and spread God's kingdom on the earth. In the Hebrew scriptures God self-identifies as the God of Abraham, Isaac and Jacob, and their descendants. God now shows a concern for all of the nations. "Thus, as Yahweh's compassion reaches out to Israel and

---

123 Miriam Jordan, "Trump Administration Ends Temporary Protection for Haitians," November 20, 2017, accessed on November 23, 2017, https://www.nytimes.com/2017/11/20/us/haitians-temporary-status.html   and Gabrielle Ware, UN Warns US to Fight Racism After Charlottesville, August 24, 2017, accessed on November 23, 2017, https://www.newsy.com/stories/un-is-alarmed-by-racist-events-in-us-gives-stern-warning/.

124 Lesslie Newbigin, *The Open Secret: An Introduction to the Theology of Mission* (Grand Rapids, MI: Wm. Eerdmans Publishing Co 1995), 34.

beyond, it gradually becomes clear that, in the final analysis, God is as concerned with the nations as with Israel."[125] Ultimately God has a desire for all people to enjoy salvation. The mission of God and the community of God converge on the issue of salvation open to people of all nations.

It is important to note the extreme contradiction to what was understood. People who had been disparaged and excluded from the faith community became welcome. Archaeological research indicates that, previously, Gentiles had only been allowed to enter into a certain portion of the temple. In Herod's temple, the Court of the Gentiles was located within the external wall, yet outside of the "inner court,"[126] where Jews would enter. A written warning reminded Jew and Gentile of the appropriate place for non-Hebrew people to congregate. It read: "No Foreigner is to go beyond the balustrade and the plaza of the temple zone whoever is caught doing so will have himself to blame for his death which will follow."[127] Hebrews, who were both Jews, and Jewish Christians, must have struggled to accept Gentiles as part of their community of faith. Both passages which form the biblical foundation of this paper give witness to God's salvific plan to the people of Israel, other nations, as well as persons who were considered ritually unclean. In Isaiah 56:7 God forecasts, "For my house will be called a house of prayer for all nations," not just Israel. Even the temple, set aside for the Jews, is a place where people of all nations will one day gather.

In Acts of the Apostles 10: 44-48, God's plan for salvation again reaches beyond the Jews to the Gentiles. The Holy Spirit, in this instance evidenced by speaking in tongues, was no longer confined to Hebrew Christians. Instead, the Holy Spirit rested on non-Hebrews. God sealed the reality that Gentiles were now legitimately a part of God's community and kingdom. The eternal purpose and mandate of God has been the redemption and salvation of humanity.

---

[125] David J. Bosch, "Reflections on the New Testament as a Missionary Document," *Transforming Mission: Paradigm Shifts in Theology of Mission.* (Maryknoll, NY: Orbis Books,1991), 19.

[126] Rusty Russell, "Temple Warning Inscription, Bible History Online, accessed on November 24, 2017, http://www.bible-history.com/archaeology/israel/temple-warning.html.

[127] Russell, "Temple Warning Inscription," Bible History Online.

God as revealed in history, is … the One who has elected
Israel. The purpose of this election is service, and when this
is withheld, election loses its meaning. Primarily Israel is to
serve the marginal in its midst: the orphan, the widow, the
poor, and the stranger.[128]

Just as Israel inherited a mantle of service, the same is true of Christian
disciples. The life of discipleship is a life of service in imitation of and
obedience to Jesus Christ. While studying at Christ Church at Oxford,
John and Charles Wesley, along with Robert Kirkham and William
Morgan, formed a study group. Their group gathered for methodical study,
devotion, and piety, and garnered the name "Methodists."[129] These young
men not only studied scriptures, they lived their faith. "These Methodists
grew in numbers and frequently served communion, fasted, had social
services, and worked with the poor and unemployed." [130]

One's understanding of theology should, in some regard, impact the
way a person approaches life. To state belief in Christ yet not imitate
Christ or live in obedience to Christ, speaks of a weak or underdeveloped
theology. The life of discipleship is one that impacts one's community
and, ultimately, the world. In his book, *Theology as Discipleship*, Keith L.
Johnson offers the following list as ways that Christians practice theology:

1. We practice theology as disciples when we measure our thinking
    and speaking about God by the person and work of Jesus Christ
    as revealed in scripture.
2. We practice theology as disciples when our thinking stays within
    the limits of our faith in Jesus Christ.
3. We practice theology as disciples when we seek to live obediently
    in the pattern of the incarnate Jesus Christ's obedience to God.

---

128 David J. Bosch, "Reflections on the New Testament as a Missionary Document."
     Transforming Mission: Paradigm Shifts in Theology of Mission. (Maryknoll, NY:
     Orbis Books, 1991), 18.
129 John Wesley. *The Holy Spirit and Power*, edited by Clare Weakley: (Alachua, FL:
     Bridge-Logos, 2003), 5.
130 John Wesley. *The Holy Spirit and Power*, edited by Clare Weakley: (Alachua, FL:
     Bridge-Logos, 2003), 5.

4. We practice theology as disciples when we do our theological work for the benefit of others.

5. We practice our theology as disciples when we use our theological work to serve the church and its missions.

6. We practice theology as disciples when we pursue both truth and unity.

7. We practice theology as disciples when we display confidence while avoiding defensiveness [131].

Christ followers, as disciples, are students whose assignment is to love God and others. The assignment includes telling others about God's love and showing that love through service and actions. This assignment includes serving as instruments of God's power and giving witness to God's kingdom on earth: a kingdom that demonstrates justice to all and righteousness. Our actions cannot live divorced from our theological understanding. One could assert that such a life indicates a belief that God is dead or no longer expects Christ followers to lead holy lives reflective of God's righteousness.

> A lack of obedience signifies that even though we may know a lot of information, we do not really know God. Theologians are especially susceptible to committing the error of thinking that knowledge of God can be divorced from a corresponding life of obedience.[132]

The Civil Rights Movement was theology in action. Informed by the knowledge of God's bent towards the oppressed, African American men and women successfully challenged legal segregation through the Montgomery Bus Boycott. In a letter to white clergymen who had criticized his civil rights work in Birmingham, Alabama, King's response reflected his theological understanding of God's mission.

> I am in Birmingham because injustice is here. Just as the prophets of the eighth century B.C. left their villages and

---

[131] Keith L. Johnson, *Theology as Discipleship*. (Downers Grove, IL: Intervarsity Press, 2015), 156-179.

[132] Keith L. Johnson, *Theology as Discipleship*. (Downers Grove, IL: Intervarsity Press, 2015), Ibid, 163.

carried their "thus saith the Lord" far beyond the boundaries of their home towns, and just as the Apostle Paul left his village of Tarsus and carried the gospel of Jesus Christ to the far corners of the Greco Roman world, so am I compelled to carry the gospel of freedom beyond my own home town. Like Paul, I must constantly respond to the Macedonian call for aid.[133]

It could be said that many Christ followers are not publicly demonstrating their faith because they don't have a clear understanding of Christian mission. Praxis does not and cannot exist apart from an understanding of or engagement with the purpose of mission. If one does not understand God's mission on earth and his or her role in it, how can that individual demonstrate the praxis? It may also be said that disciples are not engaging in demonstrating their faith due to an absence of power from the Holy Spirit. Lesslie Newbigin defines Christian mission as "proclaiming the kingdom of the Father, as sharing the life of the Son, and as bearing the witness of the Spirit," [134]

A notable similarity between the Azusa Street Revival and the stories of the Acts of the Apostles was the way in which the Holy Spirit descended on disciples with power. In both instances the Holy Spirit's presence was evident by a palpable presence of power and by speaking in different languages. The same Holy Spirit who visited the people during the first Festival of Pentecost after Jesus' Resurrection visited a new generation of people in a new location. In both situations, the gospel spread around the globe.

> ...historians would say that the Azusa Street revival played a major role in the development of modern Pentecostalism—a Movement that changed the religious landscape and became the most vibrant force for world evangelization in the 20th century.[135]

---

[133] Martin Luther King, Jr. "Letter from a Birmingham Jail," accessed February 26, 2018, https://www.africa.upenn.edu/Articles_Gen/Letter_Birmingham.html.

[134] Lesslie Newbigin, *The Open Secret: An Introduction to the Theology of Mission,* (Grand Rapids, Michigan: Wm. B. Eerdmans Publishing Co.,1995), 29.

[135] Gary B. McGee, "William J. Seymour and the Azusa Street Revival," Enrichment Journal, Springfield, MO: The General Council of the Assemblies of God. 2017, accessed on October 27, 2017, http://enrichmentjournal.ag.org/199904/026_azusa.cfm.

Our nation would benefit from a revival. Many mainline churches and denominations would benefit from a revival. All of our congregations would benefit from a new touch of Pentecost that can only be birthed by the Holy Spirit.

During the eighteenth century, John Wesley and others experienced a touch of Pentecost. Because his experience set the stage for the future Pentecostal Movement, he is considered a father of the movement. Called with the mission of bringing revival in his day, Wesley knew the person and power of the Holy Spirit. Wesley pondered the state of the church and observed the absence of the Holy Spirit's power. He asked the question, "Why is there so little evidence of spiritual gifts after the early church fathers?" His research indicated that early church fathers like Justin Martyr, Irenaeus, Tertullian, and Theophilus, Bishop of Antioch, reported miracles, healing of the sick, raising the dead and speaking in other tongues."[136] Wesley proposed the following in response: "The real cause of the loss was that the love of many, almost all of the so-called Christians had grown cold."[137]

Theology is for Everyone

What steps can be taken to turn the tide? How can congregations provide Christian believers with opportunities to better integrate their faith and action? It is important to bring others into the practice of theology. People from the pews must once again join with people in the pulpit in practicing theology. Brothers and sisters in the pews need to be allowed to "...learn theologically in ways that are easily understood contextually." Jeremiah Wright suggests we put "theology in a cup that laity can recognize."[138] The endeavor cannot be overwhelming or intimidating. Additionally, it is imperative that Christ followers engage in the development of the spiritual disciplines, so that the fire of the Holy Spirit can transform their perspective and actions. Coordinated

---

[136] John Wesley, The Holy Spirit & Power. Ed. Clare Weakly. (Alachua, FL: Bridge-Logos, 2002), 109-112.

[137] Wesley, The Holy Spirit & Power. Ed. Clare Weakly 110.

[138] Dale P. Andrews and Robert Landon Smith, Jr. Black Practical Theology. (Waco,TX: Baylor University Press, 2015), 85-87.

congregational approaches that integrate worship series, faith formation/ Sunday School, etc., can be implemented to address this concern.

It is my belief that disciple making in many Christian congregations in the US has diminished, which has resulted in or was caused by a loss of understanding of the mission of the church and a low priority for reaching new people for Christ, even the hundreds of people God brings into the building each week. A recovery of missional understanding will result in a congregation of stronger disciples who will engage and reach out to others in the pews and beyond the church walls with the good news of God's kingdom love.

FIVE

The Recovery of Mission: Revisiting and Restoring Healthy Foundations

Spiritual Assessment and Small Groups - A Strategy

WHAT IS THE SPIRITUAL TEMPERATURE of the church? What is the state of discipleship and spiritual health of the congregation? It is vitally important to assess a congregation's spiritual well-being. Churches that once included thousands of people in ministry can gradually and easily evolve to a significantly smaller community of believers that struggle to exist. Where in the life cycle of ministry does the congregation find itself? These and other related questions can be answered through a process of assessment. All ministry assessment benefits from data collection and interpretation. The data collection is often the first step. Insight and direction from the Holy Spirit are invaluable and cannot be overlooked. Some resources for assessment include Readiness 360, an online tool offered by Readiness360.org. and 'Real Discipleship Survey," from emc3coaching.com. Both are two excellent options. Organizations like "The Effective Church Group," will also work with congregations to assess current realities.

Ministry assessment benefits from a multi-faceted approach. Seeking the Lord in prayer related to the church's current reality and kingdom purpose is tantamount. A time of prayer and fasting is vital. Some pastors have utilized a process of spiritual mapping to discern and address the presence of spiritual hindrances that are blocking ministry. A question not often asked is, "are there spiritual hindrances that negatively influence congregations in their kingdom mission? That unasked and unanswered question often results in weakened ministry. The Rev. Dr. Rudy Rasmus and his wife and Co-Pastor, Juanita Rasmus, utilized spiritual mapping in their early days of ministry at St. John's Downtown (United Methodist Church) in Houston, TX.

Disciple making in many congregations has diminished. For the purposes of this book, discipleship is not equated with church membership. Discipleship is not merely Sunday worship attendance or participation at church meetings. A person can be a church member yet never experience an encounter with or power of the Living God. A member can make decisions devoid of the mind, heart or direction of God. A member can be on the roll yet not living in the anointing of the Holy Spirit.

Instead, discipleship is demonstrated in a life that is sold out to Jesus Christ. It is a lifestyle of a daily witness that reflects the Christ. Disciples are individuals who have made a commitment to know, love and follow Jesus. A disciple, who is a student, follows the instruction of their Rabbi/Teacher, Jesus. Discipleship in many congregations has diminished, which has resulted in or was caused by a loss of understanding of the mission of the church and a low priority of reaching new people for Jesus Christ. Due to the loss of missional memory, many have forgotten the importance of a discipleship lifestyle– worship, prayer, and ministry. A recovery of missional understanding will result in a congregation of stronger disciples who will engage and reach out to others in the pews and beyond the church walls with the good news of God's kingdom love.

Some might suggest that the mission of the church has changed from the early days of the Christian Church. Early Christ followers were enlisted to share the good news of God's kingdom with others. It could be said that, now, the Christian mission is solely to serve others through social services. Some believe that because many religions exist, it is no longer appropriate to push Christianity on anyone else. There must be more than one way to God. Christ can't possibly be the only way. Other challenges to missional understanding exist.

Another existing challenge is our human inclination to living in a self-reliant way instead of in dependence on the Holy Spirit. That approach is equally detrimental to congregations and individuals. Ministry devoid of the power and direction of the Holy Spirit results in stagnation and decline. A portion of the church believes that the Holy Spirit, read about in the Acts of the Apostles, no longer exists. For numerous congregations, the signs and wonders of the Holy Spirit, who spread the witness of Jesus at Pentecost and throughout all the revivals and Great Awakenings are not a possibility for their context. Therefore, separated from the Holy Spirit's power, the church has no power.

What is causing the decline? To what can we attribute the reality of individuals who are devoted church members yet who are anxious or timid about living as disciples of Jesus Christ? One cause is 'spiritual amnesia,'[139] which is a threat that confronts many mainline denomination churches. Numerous congregations filled with good and faithful members find themselves in need of church revitalization. This reality is not confined to the congregation I serve, nor to The United Methodist Church. A spiritual amnesia seems to have invaded Christian faith communities once on fire for God.

> Most churches in the United States and many in other parts
> of the world have lost their collective memories and are
> afflicted with amnesia. We no longer remember who we are
> and have forgotten the main business.[140]

This loss of missional awareness has resulted in many congregations that have cultivated members instead of disciples. The spiritual amnesia, loss of missional understanding and disconnect from theological foundations, have resulted in congregations devoid of God's power or manifestation of the gifts of God's Spirit and a low desire to reach new people with the gospel of Jesus Christ.

Pastors and congregations seeking revitalization and renewal for their ministry would benefit from engaging with practitioners and churches that have faced similar challenges. In this chapter, we will engage anthropology and explore the existence of spiritual blockages that may be impeding

---

[139] Paul Nixon, *Healing Spiritual Amnesia: Remembering What it Means to be the Church.* (Nashville, TN: Abingdon Press, 2004.) The term spiritual amnesia was borrowed from Nixon.

[140] Bob Farr with Kay Kotan, *Renovate or Die: Ten Ways to Focus Your Church on Mission.* (Nashville, TN: Abingdon Press, 2011),75.

ministry. The latter category has limited research readily accessible. Nonetheless, it is worth investigation.

It is my belief that our challenges are not caused solely by human activity or inactivity. Not much conversation exists in United Methodist circles about unseen spiritual realities that block growth and impede congregational ministry. Are there issues related to spiritual health that need to be addressed? It is my belief that spiritual issues exist that can impede congregational ministry and revitalization.

Theoretical Foundations in Ministry Practice

Congregations that have undergone revitalization provide the best resources from which other churches can learn and grow. We will engage research from various persons including United Methodist and non-United Methodist sources and will address three main categories: recovery of missional awareness, discipleship, or leader development, and becoming an externally focused congregation so that the congregation can fulfill its call to reach the multi-ethnic, multi-cultural community in which it is situated. Cookie-cutter or plug-and-play approaches are often not helpful. It is helpful to learn from proven strategies that can aid revitalization in each congregation's context.

The following are assumptions that frame this research:

- There is a need for the recovery of mission by the church.
- There has been a loss of understanding related to the mission of the local church.
- Disciple making has been replaced by the making of good church members.
- Hospitality extended toward community members and organizations often has more priority than evangelism/faith sharing.
- Attending to the work of the church is often more highly valued than attending to ministry unto the Lord—spiritual disciplines, Bible study, etc.
- Ministry emphasis is often based on maintaining and addressing the needs of those already in congregations versus inviting non-church members to join them in their faith journey with Christ.

- Maintenance of the status quo instead of "social disruption" is often the main component of the church's ministry action plan.
- Congregations often adopt an inwardly focused approach instead of an externally focused ministry and outreach approach.
- Homogeneous ministry is often the default practice instead of multi-ethnic, multi-cultural, and diverse ministry.
- Discipleship in many established congregations is a challenged reality.
- Evangelism is avoided because many believe all religions are equal and Jesus is not really needed because all paths lead to God.
- Congregations need to reach beyond the church walls to engage and love non-members and non-Christians.
- Potential existence of negative spiritual influences impeding church revitalization needs to be addressed through prayer.

Recovery of Understanding of Mission

Many United Methodist Congregations are actively in mission to their communities through soup kitchens, food pantries, and other social service ministries. These ministries touch the lives of many people. An interesting reality in many of these situations is that there is no intentional sharing of the good news. There is often no explanation of "why" the congregation and members do the good deeds. In some situations, the volunteers look negatively at a request to let people know why they do what they do.

> Many times, we Methodists do good deeds. But too often we don't let others know why we are doing the good deed. We are called to do the good deeds while sharing the good news.[141]

The mission of the Christian Church is to make disciples of Jesus Christ. All that we do is a loving extension and testimony to the mission of making disciples.

Bob Farr and Kay Kotan suggest that the United Methodist Church is not structured to reach new people for Jesus Christ. They assert that the

---

[141] Bob Farr with Kay Kotan. *Renovate or Die: Ten Ways to Focus Your Church on Mission*. (Nashville, TN: Abingdon Press, 2011), 32.

denomination is structured more to receive people than to go and reach new people. Additionally, Farr and Kotan contend that members, not disciples, are being cultivated and developed in this structure. "For better than fifty years, we, the mainline church, had produced church. We said to people, 'Come a little bit, do a little bit, give a little bit, and say a whole lot.'"[142] In this understanding, discipleship efforts are at a natural disadvantage. "Most churches were built on receiving new members, not on reaching new people."[143] Farr and Kotan correctly assert that for previous generations, brand loyalty attracted people to attend or connect with a congregation. Both of my parents were Methodists. Their parents and grandparents were active in the Methodist Episcopal Church, a predecessor to the UMC. Many of my cousins no longer live by that brand loyalty in choosing a congregation. That reality has shifted and is all but deconstructed.

Strengthen, Create, or Renew Discipleship
Opportunities through Small Groups

Small group ministry is a proven tool that continues to enhance spiritual growth and discipleship. "Class meetings and bands" were a component of the early Methodist movement and church as a means for spiritual accountability and to help people grow to spiritual maturity. Now, participation in small groups can influence the missional understanding and unified direction of an entire congregation.

> ...once we took the steps necessary to make [small groups] a genuine priority—by hiring a staff member to wake up thinking about small groups and by clarifying the expectation that all leaders would participate — the impact on the health and spiritual DNA of our church was profound and nearly immediate.[144]

Numerous congregations have successfully engaged small group processes and experienced substantial growth in membership and discipleship as

---

[142] Farr with Kotan, *Renovate or Die: Ten Ways to Focus Your Church on Mission*, 1.

[143] Bob Farr with Kay Kotan. *Renovate or Die: Ten Ways to Focus Your Church on Mission*, (Nashville, TN: Abingdon Press, 2011), 77.

[144] Larry Osborne, *Sticky Church*. (Grand Rapids, MI: Zondervan, 2008), 48.

a result. The Yoido Full Gospel Central Church in South Korea has been a leading example of small group ministry. However, Larry Osborne cautions pastors not to expect small groups to result in the exponential church growth that took place at Yoido Full Gospel Central Church. Small group ministry is not a one-size-fits-all endeavor. Affiliated with the Assemblies of God denomination, under the leadership of founding Pastor Paul David Yonggi Cho, Yoido Church grew to be the largest church in the denomination. A May 2017 article reported the congregation was approaching 800,000.[145] Osborne suggests that the small group model offered by Cho does not readily adapt to our Western society context.

Differences related to understanding of Christianity or pastoral authority are two things that prevent a plug-and-play use of that model.[146] What worked in South Korea is not going to work here. One corollary between the Yoido and North Coast Church written about by Larry Osborne, is that small group ministry enhanced the spiritual health and vitality of the congregation. Small groups or cell ministry has been shown to enhance relationships and opportunities for people to grow in faith in our times of transitory living. Small groups are vehicles that not only encourage spiritual growth of church members but also can be an effective way to reach out and include non-church members, as evidenced by the experience of Impact Church. "Connection Groups are places where healthy and positive accountability happens; where people are encouraged to submit to spiritual accountability with each other."[147] The purpose of Impact Church's Connection Groups is to provide places where people are "grounded and growing, knowing who they are, building a closer relationship with God, and strengthening their relationships with each other."[148] Rather than meet only in homes, the Connection Groups also

---

[145] "World's Largest Single Church with 800,000 members," accessed on December 13, 2017, https://www.youtube.com/watch?v=25Jpdfip8-4.

[146] Larry Osborne, *Sticky Church*. (Grand Rapids, MI: Zondervan, 2008), 142-143.

[147] Olu Brown, Impact Lead Team with Christine Shinn Latona. *Zero to 80: Innovative Ideas for Planting and Accelerating Church Growth*. (Atlanta, GA: Impact Press, 2010), 95.

[148] Olu Brown, Impact Lead Team with Christine Shinn Latona. *Zero to 80: Innovative Ideas for Planting and Accelerating Church Growth*, (Atlanta, GA: Impact Press, 2010), 95.

meet "in public places, like restaurants and coffee shops, where it is natural for people to drop in."[149]

Another variation on the small group model is the cell church model. In cell churches, cell groups "…are the basic unit and expression of the church."[150] All small group strategies don't share the same focus or function. Whereas the previous model addressed spiritual growth of members of a church, Cordle's cell groups are intrinsically externally focused. Cordle makes a distinction between small groups and cell groups. "One-way cell groups differ from other small groups is that they are fundamentally outward focused. The group's goal is to reach unreached people and lead them into a relationship with Jesus Christ."[151] For Cordle, the role of the small group, or cell, is not singularly to help current Christ followers grow in their discipleship, but also to reach new people with the gospel of Jesus Christ. The cells are outposts that, together, constitute the local church. Cordle's proposed model will not be used for this project. For the purposes of this project, the model of cell or small groups will foster spiritual growth and "relational discipleship"[152] in the vein of traditional small groups. Each model of small group ministry reports the development of disciples who, due to transformation by the renewing of their minds, recover a deeper understanding of the mission of the Church. Again, small groups will be a component of the project with the CUMC congregational leadership. Small/Cell groups will be used in the congregation after completion of the project.

Prayer is an element of revitalization that cannot be overlooked. In every move of God, there are usually counter attacks to thwart and eliminate progress. It is amazing to note numerous congregations that previously experienced strong moves of God, as evidenced by vibrant ministries and significant worship attendance, that now struggle to survive. Why? How can congregations that once had thousands in worship dwindle to below

---

149   Brown, Impact Lead Team with Christine Shinn Latona. *Zero to 80: Innovative Ideas for Planting and Accelerating Church Growth*, 97.

150   Steve Cordle, *The CHURCH in Many HOUSES: Reaching Your Community Through Cell-Based Ministry.* (Nashville, TN: Abingdon Press, 2005), 23.

151   Cordle, *The CHURCH in Many HOUSES: Reaching Your Community Through Cell-Based Ministry*, 23.

152   Dan Glover and Claudia Lavy, *Deepening Your Effectiveness: Restructuring the Local Church for Life Transformation.* (Nashville, TN: Discipleship Resources, 2006), 186.

fifty people in attendance? It is my belief that negative spiritual influences can impact congregational life including evangelism and outreach.

Dr. Brad Long, Presbyterian Reformed Ministries International, agrees:

> I have visited church after church where the Holy Spirit was demonstrably at work. Congregants were excited by their experience of the real presence of Jesus. Major growth followed and yet, after some time things seemed to fall apart. In due time these congregations found themselves enveloped in spiritual warfare, sometimes with devastating results.[153]

Long stresses the importance of addressing the human and spiritual issues appropriately. "Human causes can be addressed by human strategies. Spiritual issues must be addressed spiritually."[154] Scripture alludes to this often-unaddressed reality.

> [3] For though we live in the world, we do not wage war as the world does. [4] The weapons we fight with are not the weapons of the world. On the contrary, they have divine power to demolish strongholds. [5] We demolish arguments and every pretension that sets itself up against the knowledge of God, and we take captive every thought to make it obedient to Christ. 2 Corinthians 10: 3-5 NIV [155]

Another passage also speaks to this reality.

> For our struggle is not against flesh and blood, but against the rulers, against the authorities, against the powers of this dark world and against the spiritual forces of evil in the heavenly realms. Ephesians 6:12 NIV[156]

---

[153] Brad Long, video and script for "Discerning Strongholds in the Local Church-Introduction," Recorded February 13, 2014, accessed on December 8, 2017, http://discernwith.us/discerning-strongholds-in-the-local-church-introduction.

[154] Long, video and script for "Discerning Strongholds in the Local Church-Introduction."

[155] 2 Corinthians 10: 3-5, NIV, accessed December 14, 2017, https://www.biblegateway.com/passage/?search=2+Corinthians+10%3A+3-5&version=NIV.

[156] Ephesians 6: 12, NIV, accessed on August 19, 2022, https://www.biblegateway.com/passage/?search=Ephesians+6%3A12&version=NIV..

Long offers the following question for congregations as they assess the source or cause of the situation. "Are these things caused by evil spirits … or just the result of human sinfulness? Certainly, human sinfulness is a big part of it. In all of the cases I can name, there are people always involved."[157] Addressing spiritual issues with human responses can result in more broken relationships and fail to turn the situation around.

> We must address the question of the demonic because if it is present, then all the normal processes of dealing with conflicts (which always arise whenever two or more people try to work together) are not effective. Matthew 18 church discipline simply does not work if the demonic has a footing. Loving people, listening to them, correcting them gently as discipline to win them back to obedient discipleship will have disappointing results. The reason is, in such a case we are met by demons' intent on blocking the resolution of the problem. An entirely different sphere of engagement is thus required.[158]

In hindsight, this insight would have helped congregational revitalization efforts in some of the congregations I served previously. My attention and approach addressed human realities. I did not fully discern the spiritual as well as the human causes of challenges. "Everywhere churches are being destroyed and compromised in their witness because they are unaware of how to discern and engage both the human and spiritual dimensions of Satan's work that is intended to block the move of advance of the Gospel of Jesus Christ."[159]

The discipline of anthropology provides keen insights into research and implementation of this project. The context of the project is a multi-ethnic and multi- cultural faith community. At least six nations are represented in the congregation's constituents and members. In what ways do cultural

---

[157] Brad Long, video and script for "Discerning Strongholds in the Local Church-Introduction," Recorded February 13, 2014, accessed on December 8, 2017, http://discernwith.us/discerning-strongholds-in-the-local-church-introduction.

[158] Long, video and script for "Discerning Strongholds in the Local Church-Introduction."

[159] Brad Long, video and script for "Discerning Strongholds in the Local Church-Introduction." Recorded February 13, 2014, accessed on December 8, 2017, http://discernwith.us/discerning-strongholds-in-the-local-church-introduction.

differences impact discipleship efforts? For this paper, I'll align the secular approach of leadership development with discipleship. Both entail training of students in some regard.

Theoretical Perspectives from the Discipline of Anthropology

In the multi-ethnic, multi-cultural world in which we live, it is painfully clear that differences in perspectives and understandings exist. Perspectives and understanding are influenced by socio-cultural backgrounds. What is valued or understood in one culture may be addressed differently in another. Cultural differences can impact discipleship and leader training efforts. Anthropological models provide unique approaches to ministry.

Anthropology and religion have an interesting relationship. In the case of anthropology and world missions, the two disciplines have been strange bedfellows. "…it is not surprising that a fair amount of antagonism toward missionaries has come from anthropologists."[160] Historically, missionaries provided needed and useful information to anthropologists.

> It is noteworthy that anthropologists have been loath to recognize the great debt they owe to missionaries, not only in the early stages of anthropology's development, but even today as missionaries provide hospitality, vocabulary lists, and other aids to fledging anthropologists in the fields.[161]

Missionaries have long provided necessary ethnographic information to anthropologists. As early as the fifteenth century, Catholic missionary ethnographers' findings have provided useful research.[162] A branch of

---

[160] Darrell L. Whiteman, "One Significant Solution: How Anthropology Became the Number One Study For Evangelical Missionaries, Part 1: Anthropology and Mission: The Incarnational Connection," *International Journal of Frontier Missions,* Winter 2003. 38, accessed on December 11, 2017, http://www.ijfm. org/PDFs_IJFM/21_1_PDFs/35_44_Whiteman2.pdf., 38.

[161] Whiteman, "One Significant Solution: How Anthropology Became the Number One Study For Evangelical Missionaries, Part 1," 36.

[162] Whiteman, "One Significant Solution: How Anthropology Became the Number One Study For Evangelical Missionaries, Part 1," 36.

anthropology called ethnography "deals with the scientific description of individual cultures."[163]

While anthropology and missiology have worked together to provide cultural, ethnic, and linguistic information about people, it must be noted that anthropology and missiology have occasionally found themselves on opposite sides of current issues. In the seventeenth century, one school of anthropology substantiated belief in "the inequality of the races."[164] Later, some circles of Christians shared their belief, but, in that instance, the Evangelicals "affirmed that all of humanity was one, not diverse species, and that there were not moral or physical inequalities inherent in the human race."[165]

Just as anthropology has been taught in seminaries to train missionaries who were going to travel to other countries to serve peoples with backgrounds different from themselves, the discipline also is invaluable in orienting individuals for cross cultural, multi-cultural, and multi-ethnic ministry. Wheaton College trained numerous anthropologists to serve as missionaries, including evangelist Billy Graham, who graduated in 1943. Graham had chosen anthropology as a major partly because of an interest in becoming a missionary.[166]

Anthropological research has shed light on cultural dynamics in leader development among ethnically and culturally diverse communities. These insights are invaluable, especially for this project, in light of our

---

[163] Dictionary.com, accessed on December 11, 2017, http://www.dictionary.com/browse/ethnographer.

[164] Darrell L. Whiteman, "One Significant Solution: How Anthropology Became the Number One Study For Evangelical Missionaries, Part 1: Anthropology and Mission: The Incarnational Connection," *International Journal of Frontier Missions,* Winter 2003. 38, accessed on December 12, 2017, http://www.ijfm.org/PDFs_IJFM/21_1_PDFs/35_44_Whiteman2.pdf., 38.

[165] Darrell L. Whiteman, "One Significant Solution: How Anthropology Became the Number One Study For Evangelical Missionaries, Part 1: Anthropology and Mission: The Incarnational Connection," *International Journal of Frontier Missions,* Winter 2003. 38, accessed on December 12, 2017, http://www.ijfm.org/PDFs_IJFM/21_1_PDFs/35_44_Whiteman2.pdf., 38.

[166] Darrell Whiteman, *Anthropology and Mission: An Uneasy Journey Toward Mutual Understanding, Paradigm Shifts in Christian Witness: Insights from Anthropology, Communication, and Spiritual Power.* (Maryknoll, NY: Orbis Books, 2008), 9.

multi-cultural, multi-ethnic context. Alan R. Johnson offers his experience obtained from his research training leaders in Thailand. "Because I wanted to be sensitive to cultural dynamics, I chose an anthropological approach using participant observation to seek a holistic understanding of the social influence processes operating in the community that I studied."[167] Johnson encourages people to be culturally sensitive to those with whom they work. Without identification of cultural dynamics, what misunderstandings have or would occur in efforts to cultivate and nurture multi-ethnic, multi-cultural congregational leadership? The intent of Johnson's work "…is to stimulate and provoke the thinking of those who are involved in training leaders, either within or without of their own sociocultural setting, to explore new or adjusted methodologies in their training that take seriously the role of cultural dynamics in the conduct of leadership."[168]

What implicit biases or perceptions exist in a faith community of individuals from various backgrounds? At the initial writing of this text, which served as my Doctor of Ministry project, members of the church I served as pastor reflected ethnic and cultural diversity. Church members and constituent backgrounds were - Chinese, Sri Lankan, Nigerian, Japanese, Liberian, African American, European American and Hispanic/Latino.

Johnson offers a few strategies that are transferrable to the congregational context. They are:

1. Leadership must be understood in its sociocultural context.
   a. Seek to understand the socio-cultural context of the leaders.
   b. As we strive to teach or train we must be listeners and learners ourselves.

2. Leadership practice is primarily non-discursive.

---

[167] Alan R. Johnson. "An Anthropological Approach to the Study of Leadership: Lessons learned on improving leadership practice." *Transformation 24/3 July & October 2007*, 214, accessed December 12, 2017, http://thaimissions.info/gsdl/collect/thaimiss/index/assoc/HASH468a.dir/doc.pdf

[168] Alan R. Johnson. "An Anthropological Approach to the Study of Leadership: Lessons learned on improving leadership practice." *Transformation 24/3 July & October 2007*, 214, accessed December 12, 2017, http://thaimissions.info/gsdl/collect/thaimiss/index/assoc/HASH468a.dir/doc.pdf.

a. In the case of the study, the most appropriate approach for the community required more of a direct, focused presentation of information.

b. This approach engages cognitive anthropology, which takes into consideration "different types of processing used with explicit and implicit knowledge."

3. "Leadership training should be an intentional process, rooted in dialogue conducted over time."

a. In order to teach "someone how to be a good leader we must understand what good leadership looks and functions like in that particular socio-cultural setting."

b. Pay attention to the implicit, unspoken understandings and beliefs. They influence community interactions.

c. Do not discount the importance of understanding the context of the leadership.[169]

In the process of researching the correlation of the discipline of anthropology and this project, an interesting development was the revelation of differences in perceptions of the spiritual world among people of various cultural backgrounds. Seminary professor, Tormod Engelsviken experienced the differences in perceptions of people of the West and Two-Thirds World firsthand. "There is a severe difference in worldview and understanding of the spiritual realities and spiritual conflict between the church's ministry in the Western world and that of the Two-Thirds World,"[170] Tormod Engelsviken explained.

A Norwegian, Engelsviken traveled to Ethiopia to teach systematic theology at a seminary. His students asked him questions for which he had no answer at that time. Students began asking him for direction on

---

[169] Alan R. Johnson. "An Anthropological Approach to the Study of Leadership: Lessons learned on improving leadership practice." *Transformation 24/3 July & October 2007*, 216-221, accessed December 12, 2017, http://thaimissions.info/gsdl/collect/thaimiss/index/assoc/HASH468a.dir/doc.pdf.

[170] Tormod Engelsviken. *Spiritual Conflict: A Challenge for the Church in the West with a View to the Future. Paradigm Shifts in Christian Witness: Insights from Anthropology, Communication and Spiritual Power.* (Maryknoll, NY: Orbis Books, 2008), 118.

how to help people who were oppressed by evil spirits. His theological education excluded training related to "Satan and evil spirits [and] the practice of casting them out of possessed people..."[171] He encountered similar experiences in China and learned that other Western theologians encountered "spiritual conflict" and differences in experiences with people in the Two-Thirds World.

His insights from participation at the Lausanne Theology and Strategy Group consultation in Kenya, entitled "Deliver Us from Evil," are helpful for this project and paper. Thirty people from various parts of the world attended this conference. Some of his insights are:

- "The whole theological and missiological area of spiritual conflict may be one where the church in the West has most to learn from churches in the Global South."[172]
- Evil, or spiritual conflict, is not something to be contended with only outside of the West. It is often an unseen, unrecognized, unaddressed reality in Western Christianity, in the United States, and Europe.
- The Enlightenment and development of science and empiricism have contributed to the Westernized belief that evil does not exert influence in people's lives or communities.[173]
- Satan is real and actively opposes the work of the church and God's kingdom advances.[174]

---

[171] Tormod Engelsviken. *Spiritual Conflict: A Challenge for the Church in the West with a View to the Future. Paradigm Shifts in Christian Witness: Insights from Anthropology, Communication and Spiritual Power,* (Maryknoll, NY: Orbis Books, 2008), 116.

[172] Engelsviken. *Spiritual Conflict: A Challenge for the Church in the West with a View to the Future. Paradigm Shifts in Christian Witness: Insights from Anthropology, Communication and Spiritual Power.,* 118.

[173] Engelsviken. *Spiritual Conflict: A Challenge for the Church in the West with a View to the Future. Paradigm Shifts in Christian Witness: Insights from Anthropology, Communication and Spiritual Power,* 118.

[174] Engelsviken. *Spiritual Conflict: A Challenge for the Church in the West with a View to the Future. Paradigm Shifts in Christian Witness: Insights from Anthropology, Communication and Spiritual Power,* 118.

Englesviken asks, "Has the Enlightenment influenced the Western culture and congregations so much that both have discarded the spiritual realm?" In many regards, I believe the answer is yes. Personal pastoral experience provided glimpses of spiritual evil in congregational settings. Once, while serving another church, there was a meeting in my office. During this meeting, a few of us heard a snake's hiss. No snake was in the office. One evening, while sleeping, I was awakened from sleep by a dream of contorted faces in the ceiling of the church sneering at me. My seminary education did not teach me to discern and engage in spiritual warfare.

It is my belief that spiritual barriers influence congregations. Why else would Christians block efforts to share the gospel with people outside the church walls? Like others, I had not received training in seminary to discern or adequately address the reality of spiritual hindrances.

Englesviken shared research which indicates that, while Western Christians may not have an understanding of the spiritual realm, there is an increased acknowledgement of belief in spirits in Norway's secular society. "In a recent poll in Norway, one of the most secularized nations in Europe, twenty-two percent expressed the belief that it is possible to get in contact with the spirits of deceased persons. This is an increase of six percent from 1998."[175] Another example of the growth of belief by the secular world in the existence of the spiritual world is a prime-time show in Denmark and Norway entitled, "The Power of the Spirits." Although not the only persons to deal with evil, clergy were called in to address the evil. "Pastors in the Lutheran church in Norway are frequently called to houses with 'unrest' to pray and expel evil or bothersome forces. A special liturgy has been developed for this procedure."[176] The United States is also experiencing a similar phenomenon as evidenced by television programming like "Supernatural" and "Paranormal Witness."

---

[175] Tormod Engelsviken. *Spiritual Conflict: A Challenge for the Church in the West with a View to the Future. Paradigm Shifts in Christian Witness: Insights from Anthropology, Communication and Spiritual Power,* (Maryknoll, NY: Orbis Books, 2008), 124.

[176] Tormod Engelsviken. *Spiritual Conflict: A Challenge for the Church in the West with a View to the Future. Paradigm Shifts in Christian Witness: Insights from Anthropology, Communication and Spiritual Power,* (Maryknoll, NY: Orbis Books, 2008), 124.

If houses and people can be under the influence of evil spirits, can congregations also experience similar situations? If so, how can that reality be recognized and addressed? In an Enlightened worldview and understanding, this would not be a reality and would therefore not require any attention. That reasoning is faulty. It is my contention that many congregations are struggling with Satanic oppression that is unchecked and directly blocking or impeding God's kingdom advances and inhibiting church growth and discipleship efforts. For many congregations and congregational leaders, this is not even a consideration. What price do we pay for not acknowledging the possibility?

> It seems quite clear that spiritual conflict is an urgent task for the church and its pastoral leaders both in the Global South and in the West. This comes as no surprise. If Satan and his demons and the whole spiritual realm have ontological reality and can actively influence the lives of people, culture, religions, and political and economic structures, they cannot be relegated to a premodern time or to specific ("animistic") cultures. They are real and active ... All churches need a renewed study of the biblical worldview and the practice of spiritual conflict.[177]

Early Methodism had a different understanding of the spiritual realm. John Wesley understood the Christian life and walk to be one of a battle. Contrary to the teachings of the Enlightenment, John Wesley believed in the existence of angels and demons. "While the influence of Enlightenment was significant, it did not seem to substantially influence Wesley's demonology or his belief in the miraculous in general."[178] While many of the spiritual descendants of Wesley in the Western World do not believe in or acknowledge the possibility of a spiritual battle, Wesley understood that each Christian faced spiritual battles.

"Wesley insisted on the pervasive influence of spiritual powers, both benevolent and malevolent, in the daily affairs of human beings.

---

[177] Engelsviken. *Spiritual Conflict: A Challenge for the Church in the West with a View to the Future. Paradigm Shifts in Christian Witness: Insights from Anthropology, Communication and Spiritual Power*, 125.

[178] Jeffrey Williams, *Religion and Violence in Early American Methodism: Taking the Kingdom by Force.* (Bloomington, IN: Indiana University Press, 2010), 27.

Wesley testified to horrifying demonic possessions, cases of witchcraft, and miraculous wonders, begging skeptics to account for these through scientific or natural means."[179] In the current times in which we live, it appears that many people in the church discount the spiritual reality of life. "...People don't understand there is a spiritual realm."[180]

While it is not my intent to contend that there is a demon behind every pew, it is my belief that, in some settings, evil exacts unseen, unaddressed influence in congregations that impacts discipleship, church growth, and God's kingdom advances in the parish. If that is the case, many congregations don't even know they are in a battle. How should congregations address the situation?

Some would recommend spiritual mapping as an approach to identifying and addressing negative spiritual influences. George Otis explained that Spiritual Mapping is "nothing more ethereal than creating a spiritual profile of a community based on careful research. It is a tool, he says, for intelligent prayer aimed at opening spiritually blind eyes to the gospel."[181] The idea of spiritual mapping has garnered many supporters and critics. Some individuals have suggested that personal homes and churches can benefit from a spiritual housecleaning. Gary Maupin teaches that spiritual housecleaning is necessary to rid locations from evil influences. "When there is an unwanted spiritual presence or curse on your house, on your car, on your farm, in your church or in you, and it needs to be removed...it will free you up to worship freely and help others,"[182] Maupin explains.

Maupin illustrates his belief based on the example of Achan, who after a battle deceptively kept something God instructed the Israelites to destroy. (Josh. 7: 10-12)

---

[179] Williams, *Religion and Violence in Early American Methodism: Taking the Kingdom by Force)*, 27.

[180] Gary Maupin, "Spiritual Housecleaning," Video, Part 1 of 4, accessed on December 13, 2017, http://www.whereheleadsme.org/teaching-videos.html.

[181] Art Moore, "Church Growth: Spiritual Mapping Gains Credibility Among Leaders," *Christianity Today.* January 12, 1998, accessed on December 13, 2017, http://www.christianitytoday.com/ct/1998/january12/8t1055.html.

[182] Gary Maupin, "Spiritual Housecleaning," Video, Part 1 of 4, accessed December 13, 2017, http://www.whereheleadsme.org/teaching-videos.html.

¹⁰ The Lord said to Joshua, "Stand up! What are you doing down on your face?¹¹ Israel has sinned; they have violated my covenant, which I commanded them to keep. They have taken some of the devoted things; they have stolen, they have lied, they have put them with their own possessions. ¹²That is why the Israelites cannot stand against their enemies; they turn their backs and run because they have been made liable to destruction. I will not be with you anymore unless you destroy whatever among you is devoted to destruction.¹⁸³ Joshua 7: 10-12 NIV

In this situation, God communicated an unwillingness to help them because of the items that had been devoted to other gods. Maupin explains that such rebellion opens a door to evil presence. If indeed something is present that honors another deity or dishonors God, there potentially is a problem that can thwart ministry. Another scripture, Deut. 7: 25-26, sheds light on possible reasons that congregations struggle.

²⁵ The images of their gods you are to burn in the fire. Do not covet the silver and gold on them, and do not take it for yourselves, or you will be ensnared by it, for it is detestable to the Lord your God. ²⁶ Do not bring a detestable thing into your house or you, like it, will be set apart for destruction. Regard it as vile and utterly detest it, for it is set apart for destruction.¹⁸⁴ Deuteronomy 7: 25-26 NIV

Again, Maupin and others recommend a spiritual housecleaning as a means to address the issue(s). Maupin recommends:

1. First make sure the location contains no physical items that displease God. He offered the following items that invite evil in. Included in his list of items to avoid were games like 'Dungeons and Dragons', anything attached to Hinduism and Buddhism, Yoga, books like Harry Potter, and astrology.¹⁸⁵

---

¹⁸³ Joshua 7: 10-12, Bible Gateway. Accessed December 13, 2017, https://www.biblegateway.com/passage/?search=Joshua+7&version=NIV.

¹⁸⁴ Deuteronomy 7: 25-26, NIV, Bible Gateway, accessed December 14, 2017, https://www.biblegateway.com/passage/?search=Deuteronomy+7:25-26.

¹⁸⁵ Gary Maupin, "Spiritual Housecleaning," Videos- Part 1, 2,3 & 4, accessed December 13, 2017, http://www.whereheleadsme.org/teaching-videos.html.

2. Enlist a group of individuals to pray for God to reveal any item that needs to be destroyed or a situation that needs to be addressed. The team should include pastoral and intercessory teams and address subjective and objective information that surfaces.[186]

    a. The teams are encouraged to be open to subjective information, such as the spiritual gift of words of knowledge provided by the Holy Spirit.

    b. Another source of information hails from verifiable information—historical, etc., which forms the corpus of objective information.[187]

3. Proceed with caution. Enter into a time of prayer and fasting to best discern how God is directing next steps.[188] One person has cautioned, 'Diagnosis of a problem doesn't necessarily mean assignment.'[189] Make sure God wants you to address the situation.

One may wonder if it is possible for an item or human interaction such as violence, deception, etc., within a congregation, to negatively impact a ministry. Why would God be so concerned? The situation couldn't actually have such serious implications that ministry would be impacted negatively. The reality of unaddressed spiritual challenges may be more pervasive than imagined. In this process, it is important for members of the teams to confess personal sins to God. Items giving homage to other gods can't be welcomed in God's church.

Increasingly, elements of the New Age Movement are creeping into Christian churches. For example, what are the implications of churches that provide space for a yoga class from an external organization or offer a church sponsored yoga or Tai Chi class? It could be said that yoga and or Tai Chi don't pose any challenge to the ministry of a congregation. Why

---

186 Eddie and Alice Smith. *Spiritual Housecleaning: Protect Your Home and Family from Spiritual Pollution.* (Bloomington, MN: Chosen Books, 2015), 170-171.

187 Smith. *Spiritual Housecleaning: Protect Your Home and Family from Spiritual Pollution,* 170-171.

188 Eddie and Alice Smith. *Spiritual Housecleaning: Protect Your Home and Family from Spiritual Pollution,* (Bloomington, MN: Chosen Books, 2015), 170-181.

189 Smith. *Spiritual Housecleaning: Protect Your Home and Family from Spiritual Pollution,* 183.

would God care about either of them? Their purpose is exercise, increased breathing, nothing else. They have no spiritual connections. Those classes are harmless. Everything is not permissible in God's churches. Some situations exist that have spiritual implications that can negatively impact ministry.

The following scenario is not something I heard about but witnessed personally. A well-loved and attended community yoga class is held in a church classroom on an upper floor of a church. The classroom hosts a variety of images including a photo of the sitting Buddha and an engraving containing the "Om." Upon first sight, all looks innocent, yet that is not the case. A deeper look uncovers unseen challenges. In an article entitled, '5 things to know about Om,' it is explained that "The word Om is defined by Hindu scripture as being the primordial sound of creation."[190] That sound, made during each, class has spiritual implications. "Broken down, the three letters of A-U-M represent a number of sacred trinities," including the deities in charge of creation, preservation, and destruction of the universe – Brahma, Vishnu, and Shiva." [191] Each time yoga class participants chanted the 'Om' three Hindu gods were represented and honored, in a building of Christian worship. This room is situated in the classroom on the highest level of the church, above the sanctuary, for 16 years. The chant created an "altar" of sorts honoring 3 Hindu gods. To complicate matters, a Tai Chi class was also taught in the narthex for many years. Eastern Religions had stealthily entered the premises.

What doors of spiritual interference were opened in the life of this congregation? What permissions were granted to the Enemy to block God's kingdom making through the congregation? Through ignorance, decisions were made which dishonored the heart and character of God and idolatry was introduced to the church. A decision made in ignorance does not excuse the sin or consequence.

---

[190] "5 things to know about Om."Hindu American, accessed May 31, 2022. https://www.hinduamerican.org/blog/5-things-to-know-about-om#:~:text=The%20word%20Om%20is%20defined,vibrations%20are%20able%20to%20manifest.

[191] 5 things to know about Om."Hindu American, accessed May 31, 2022. https://www.hinduamerican.org/blog/5-things-to-know-about-om#:~:text=The%20word%20Om%20is%20defined,vibrations%20are%20able%20to%20manifest.

In situations like these, spiritual housecleaning of the church is necessary. After the first steps of the spiritual housecleaning take place, other recommendations exist. The following list, offered by Eddie and Alice Smith, includes some potential next actions:

1. The pastor(s) and a small team of leaders pray prayers of repentance and replacement. An example of a replacement prayer is "Lord cleanse us from the sin of sexual promiscuity and make us a people of sexual purity."[192]
2. Anoint the doors and windows of the church and dedicate it, once again, to the Lord.
3. Create "a covenant of love, stating the purpose of the church. Have members sign it into the church's legal records."[193]
4. Entire congregations have had a night of commitment, signing a document of commitment to God.
5. Gather and pray prayers of dedication on the corners of the property.

Interestingly enough, a year after the yoga classes began meeting in the space, a significant and recurring leak in the hallway over the stairwell leading to the room, developed. During the 15 years, numerous repair attempts were made. The leak always returned. It was not until the Yoga studio had vacated the space and premises, that the leak situation ceased. Even in the presence of heavy, driving rain, the leak has not returned. Additionally, after the departure of the studio, there was a lifting in the atmosphere experienced in worship services and an increased commitment to participation in bible study and corporate mid-week prayer.

A Word of Warning

God is a jealous God and will not abide his people following after other gods, knowingly or unknowingly. That includes us. What, if any

---

[192] Smith. *Spiritual Housecleaning: Protect Your Home and Family from Spiritual Pollution*. 182.

[193] Eddie and Alice Smith. *Spiritual Housecleaning: Protect Your Home and Family from Spiritual Pollution*. (Bloomington, MN: Chosen Books, 2015), 182.

consequences, exist for idolatry? In Exodus 20, we enter into the mind and heart of God related to the issue of idolatry.

> And God spoke all these words: ² "I am the LORD your God, who brought you out of Egypt, out of the land of slavery. ³ "You shall have no other gods before[a] me. ⁴ "You shall not make for yourself an image in the form of anything in heaven above or on the earth beneath or in the waters below. ⁵ You shall not bow down to them or worship them; for I, the LORD your God, am a jealous God, punishing the children for the sin of the parents to the third and fourth generation of those who hate me, ⁶ but showing love to a thousand generations of those who love me and keep my commandments. ¹⁹⁴ Exodus 20: 2-6 NIV

Even in the presence of God's grace, sin's consequences exist, even for churches.

Hindrances Must Be Addressed

Why do many churches lack power? Why is revival not breaking out the way it should — even after much prayer, effort, and strategy? Unaddressed spiritual problems may be a source of hindrances plaguing the church's efforts for growth, evangelism and community transformation for Jesus Christ. The particular situation may not be as glaring as the ones highlighted earlier, yet detrimental all the same.

What are we to do? Pray as if everything depends on God and contact people who can help you. In this situation, two contacts were invaluable. Early in the process of discernment, I contacted Rev. Dr. Laura Henry Harris author of numerous books including *Kingdom Citizenship Now: Experiencing God's Kingdom on Earth as it is In Heaven*. A founding member of Where He Leads Me Ministry, Henry Harris shared her experience pastoring a congregation that was experiencing a spiritual blockage. The best wisdom she shared was that I was to pray to understand exactly what God wanted me to do in the situation and not to get ahead of God. To get ahead of God could prove dangerous. She also recommended that

---

¹⁹⁴ Exodus 20: 1-6, accessed on June 1, 2022, https://www.biblegateway.com/passage/?search=Exodus%2020%3A1-6&version=NIV

I ask numerous people to pray for my protection and direction. The other person God used to help the efforts at the church was Rebecca Greenwood, Co-Founder, Christian Harvest International and of the Strategic Prayer Apostolic Network. She also is the author of numerous books including *Let Our Children Go: Steps to Free Your Child from Evil Influences and Demonic Harassment.* In our call she listened to the situation as I understood it, shared what she discerned and provided insights into how to pray strategically to disarm and dismantle the hindering demonic presence and interference. Her discernment confirmed much of what I thought and gave invaluable insight about other plans of the Enemy about the congregation and my family. The work did not end after the completion of my Doctor of Ministry project and reception of my Doctoral Degree. The work continues even now. After the completion of my Doctor of Ministry Degree contact was made with a clergy colleague, the Rev. Angela Kitrell, to request that she come to the church, visit the space used by the yoga studio so that she could pray in the space with me and share what she discerned.

Disciple making in many congregations has diminished, which has resulted in or was caused by a loss of understanding of the mission of the church and a low priority for reaching new people for Christ, even the myriad of people in the surrounding community. A recovery of missional understanding will result in a congregation of stronger disciples who will engage and reach out to others in the pews and beyond the church walls with the good news of God's kingdom love.

Spiritual amnesia, loss of missional awareness and spiritual blockages are serious matters which confront many congregations. The long-term implications of their presence are devastating, resulting in a congregation that is not fulfilling its mission in the community and members who don't know or understand their personal God assignment. The mission of Christian congregations is to make disciples of Jesus Christ for the transformation of the world.

My research, gleaned from the experiences of practitioners and others involved in congregational revitalization, suggests that increased and intentional opportunities for spiritual development and discipleship enhance a person's understanding of missional awareness. This suggestion correlates with the early Methodist movement's process of bands and societies. It was in those settings that spiritual accountability took place and people had opportunities to grow in their faith. Just as spiritual accountability and growth were important before, they are true now.

The project that was implemented as part of my Doctor of Ministry project, integrated a small group component that first engaged leaders, reminded, or taught them about God's mission for the local congregation, so that the congregation could become more externally focused and better connect with neighbors and the hundreds of individuals who enter the building each week to attend community meetings. The leaders were enlisted to engage others within the congregation, who then were asked to reach others outside the church building.

The discipline of anthropology will be an asset in the intentional multi-cultural, multi-ethnic ministry this congregation is called into in the Cheverly community. Failing to consider the diverse perspectives and understandings of the people who are part of the congregation can negatively impact interaction among leaders and the congregation as a whole. Anthropology can help identify implicit socio-ethnic or ethnographic realities that are present yet not acknowledged.

It is clear to me that the spiritual health of the congregation cannot be ignored as efforts are made to address spiritual amnesia and the loss of missional awareness. To ignore the spiritual health—i.e. unaddressed spiritual hindrances—is tantamount to putting a Band Aid on a deep wound. Total healing may not take place. Infection may set in. Congregational revitalization efforts may begin but not result in total transformation if barriers are not dismantled.

SIX

Project Analysis

———— ⌁ ————

God to the Church, "Do You Know Who You Are?

WHAT HAPPENS WHEN A CHURCH loses an understanding of its mission and purpose? If mission and sense of purpose drive focus and direction, a congregation with a misguided or mistaken understanding of its God assignment can be headed in the wrong direction. A church with an impaired identity can lose connection with God, its reason for being, its mission and purpose. Just as congregations can have an impaired identity, so can Christians. What happens when Christians do not live out God's assignment in the life of their communities? Many mainline denominations face this dilemma in which congregations and individual Christ followers no longer grasp who they were created to be.

In the congregational setting for this project, people faithfully serve on committees and regularly attend committee meetings. Numerous individuals volunteer in the food pantry, make sandwiches for a community feeding ministry and support children and families at the community elementary school. It is my observation that many do not actively attend to their growth as disciples corporately. It appears that many do not actively invite other individuals into a life transforming relationship with Jesus Christ. To illustrate this reality, Cheverly United Methodist Church provides meeting space for numerous community organizations resulting in hundreds of individuals entering the building each week. Although God brings hundreds of people into its church, the congregation seems to have forgotten that God is calling them to share God's love, not just the building, with guests so that they too can be invited into a life of discipleship.

Discipleship and disciple-making are to the Christian and Church what food and water are to the sustenance of life. What happens when the purpose of ministry is either forgotten or abandoned? If discipleship and disciple-making are not prioritized or actualized, ministry is greatly impacted. For many congregations, there seems to be a disconnect between the understanding of discipleship and church membership.

Church membership is not the same as discipleship. The terms Christian, disciple and church member do not share the same meaning. Being identified as a Christian is not the same as being a church member. The identification as a Christian disciple carries the distinction of following the life, teachings, and lordship of Jesus Christ. The life of a Christian is one in relationship with Jesus Christ. Christians ideally are disciples of Jesus Christ. For numerous individuals, the term Christian is synonymous with the phrase church membership. It can be said that church membership has evolved more into attendance at church meetings, than about Christians living in connection to Christ.

While the mission of the church is to "make disciples of Jesus Christ for the transformation of the world," other issues compete with its fulfillment. Facility maintenance and financial challenges preempt and displace the importance of faith formation and making disciples. Church facilities and administration are important. If attendance indicates a sense of importance, church meetings have more participation than faith formation opportunities – Bible studies, small groups, Sunday School or prayer meetings. The answer may lie in the congregation's understanding of its mission in the community. The research project is designed to investigate the premise that a congregation that is growing in its discipleship will live out an understanding of mission and ministry that intentionally strives to bring people into relationship with Jesus Christ.

Borrowing from the imagery of plants, it is as if the church has lost its connection to its spiritual roots, heritage and calling. A church, like plants, obtains nutrition from its roots. Apart from the spiritual rootedness in Jesus Christ, nurtured through the working of the Holy Spirit in our lives, intentional faith formation and an understanding of God's kingdom mandate, discipleship will not exist, and congregations will continue to die on the vine.

Disciples and congregations benefit from the rooted relationship with Jesus Christ. Apart from a growing and vibrant relationship with our Triune God, we can do nothing. Too often congregations have mistaken the administrative, day-to-day workings of maintaining the church facility and programming as the raison d'être. Ministry is so much more than that. Relationship in connection with Christ is imperative in our quest to faithfully fulfill the church's mission.

> "I am the true vine, and my Father is the gardener. ²He cuts off every branch in me that bears no fruit, while every branch that does bear fruit he prunes[a] so that it will be even more fruitful. ³You are already clean because of the word I have spoken to you. ⁴Remain in me, as I also remain in you. No branch can bear fruit by itself; it must remain in the vine. Neither can you bear fruit unless you remain in me. ⁵"I am the vine; you are the branches. If you remain in me and I in you, you will bear much fruit; apart from me you can do nothing. ⁶If you do not remain in me, you are like a branch that is thrown away and withers; such branches are picked up, thrown into the fire, and burned.[195] John 15: 1-6, NIV

Separated from its spiritual roots with God and God's kingdom mandate, the congregation and individual believer have, in some regards, disconnected from the purpose for being. Ministry fruitfulness, in this instance, has been negatively impacted. That means that even if a church is a place where many in the community meet, yet does not engage the people God brings into the building in ways that invite them into relationship with Jesus Christ, it misses opportunities for fruitfulness.

This project set out to provide opportunities for congregational leadership to shift from the mindset of "member" to "disciple" and to work to develop intentional bridge building to provide on and off ramps for people in the community to participate in the life of the congregational ministry. By reconnecting leaders with their personal and congregational God mandate and purpose, this project hoped to help people overcome "spiritual amnesia" and remind them of their God assignment in Cheverly, MD.

---

[195] John 15: 1-6, New International Version, accessed August 12, 2022, https://www.biblegateway.com/passage/?search=John+15%3A+1-6&version=NIV

It is my hypothesis that disciple making in this congregation has diminished which has resulted in or was caused by a loss of understanding of the mission of the church and a low priority for reaching new people for Christ, even the hundreds of people God brings into our building each week. The solution to this situation is the formation of Christian leaders who gain a new or renewed understanding of the mission of the church, and their role in making disciples of Jesus Christ for the transformation of the world. These leaders can influence the rest of the congregation to be transformed into action. The church leaders are enlisted to co-labor in the ministry of church revitalization.

Methodology

The methodology used for this research project included the following:

1. Pre-research survey
2. Post-research survey
3. Chapter questionnaires included in the project book – *Shift 2.0: Helping Congregations Back into the Game of Effective Ministry* by Phil Maynard
4. Sunday, after church sessions to share a meal, discuss book chapter and church visit insights
5. Church visits to area congregations to ascertain best practices from churches that have gone through or working through revitalization
6. Closing Retreat Session to review learnings from the research project
7. Shift Sermon Series -Although not included in the original proposal, I added a sermon series entitled, "Shift." Based on the chapter titles of Maynard's book, Shift 2.0, Helping Churches Back into the Game of Effective Ministry, the sermon titles, dates and scripture focus were as follows:

October 21, 2018 – "Shift: From Serve Us to Service" Matthew 25: 44-45

October 28, 2018 – "Shift: It's a Lifestyle Worship from An Event to Worship as a Lifestyle" (Romans 12:1)

November 4, 2018 Shift: Its Not all About Us (John 15: 9-12)

November 11, 2018 Shift: From Just Surviving to Thriving (Proverbs 22:9)

November 25, 2018 Shift: A Change in Perspective (Ephesians 4: 14-15)

Concerned that a smaller than expected number of church leadership had completed the survey and signed up to participate in this research project, and that the lower level of participation could diminish the project's ability to influence the congregation, I incorporated the sermon series. Also, Leadership Council members who did not participate in the project were invited and encouraged to read the book. This approach was chosen to enhance experiential learning of the research project participants. The following have been identified as learning styles [196]:

Visual
Aural
Physical
Verbal
Social
Solitary
Logical

This project engaged all of them. The process was designed to help foster transformation in the participant thought processes and hopefully actions. It was not enough for the book, sermon series or leadership team from another church to share information. In my opinion, the project would provide enough opportunity for each person to have sufficient information to come to his or her own conclusions about the need to make changes. The experiential approach helps people see things for themselves. The church visits were an invaluable component of the process for that reason. "If you want to give people a vision for creating a world-class process for intentional hospitality, take them to a church that is doing this well. If you want to create a vision for providing a life-changing youth ministry, visit a youth ministry that is thriving."[197]

---

[196] Learning Styles," accessed December 7, 2018. https://learning-styles-online.com/overview/.

[197] Phil Maynard, *Shift 2.0: Helping Congregations Back into the Game of Effective Ministry* (Knoxville, TN: Market Square Publishing Company, LLC, 2018), 223.

Project Implementation

To address this hypothesis, the project invited the twenty-one members of the Church's administrative body - the Leadership Council, the Minister of Music and Ministry Intern, to participate in a seven-week process of Bible engagement, book study, church visits and group discussions about learnings and implications for ministry at Cheverly United Methodist Church. Two other staff persons, the Facilities Manager and Treasurer serve on the Leadership Council. The Leadership Council is comprised of a representative of each ministry team. In some cases, the ministry team is led by co-chairs. The invited group represented a cross section of individuals related to culture/ethnicity, age and gender. Two young adults and one youth are part of this ministry round table. The research project participants were asked to take a pre-research and post-research survey.

These individuals were selected due to their ministry roles and responsibilities in the church. According to ¶ 252.1. of the Discipline of The United Methodist Church, the purpose of the Church Council is as follows:

1. Purpose - The church council shall provide for planning and implementing a program of nurture, outreach, witness, and resources in the local church. It shall also provide for the administration of its organization and temporal life. It shall envision, plan, implement, and annually evaluate the mission and ministry of the church. The church council shall be amenable to and function as the administrative agency of the charge conference (¶ 244). [198]

Jesus did not start his ministry working with large crowds. Instead he invited a small number of twelve men (and some women) to journey in ministry with Him. It was these individuals that Jesus taught about the nature of God, God's kingdom mandate and their role in God's kingdom. Jesus was the Rabbi and those with him were his disciples. The model used for this research project modeled Jesus' approach. A small

---

[198] "What We Believe," accessed November 23, 2018. http://www.umc.org/what-we-believe/para-252-the-church-council.

number of individuals were invited into a process and time of mentored teaching, experiential learning, and discernment. It was this small cadre of individuals who were later charged with the responsibility of sharing what they learned as they imitated their teacher and spread the good news about God's kingdom on earth.

The members of the Leadership Council are a small group of leaders who, for all intents and purposes, have been called to serve as Jesus' modern-day disciples. Tasked with implementing the nurture, outreach, and witness ministries of the church, the Leadership Council administers the life of the congregation. Although strong in their administrative roles and responsibilities, the aspect of following Jesus' lead in disciple-making is all but forgotten. Could it be that they did not know the discipleship component of their ministry roles? Was it that the church had forgotten or abandoned that element of ministry? This research project was designed to investigate the causes of the lack of discipleship and disciple-making and provide participants with opportunities to recover an understanding of God's mission for them. If church leadership could learn or regain an understanding of their individual and corporate mission of the church, they could grow in their discipleship and then share that knowledge with others in the congregation. Their participation would hopefully result in positive influence in the entire congregation so that the church's culture could shift to embrace a lifestyle of discipleship and increase evangelism to actively engage the many community members who meet in the building each week.

Of the twenty-one persons who were invited, twelve completed the pre-research project survey. That group of persons included the following members of the Leadership Council:

- Leadership Council Co-Chair-
- Trustee Team Co-Chair
- Facilities Manager (Staff Member)
- Finance Team Co-Chair
- Ministry Intern (with responsibility for Youth Ministry)
- Minister of Music
- Treasurer (Staff Member)
- Trustee Co-Chair

- United Methodist Women President/Outreach Chair
- Worship Planning Team Member
- Youth Representative
- Pastor

Nine individuals attended the first gathering. Each meeting, except the closing retreat, took place for an hour after church on Sunday. A family funeral conflicted with the date of the scheduled retreat, resulting in a change of date and format. Originally planned as a half-day experience to be held offsite at another church, the closing retreat was a 2-2 ½ hour meal at an area restaurant in a special room. Time constraints caused another change from the original proposal. The original proposal included a planned group mission experience. Schedules just wouldn't permit it. The research project implementation started later than anticipated due to slow participant responses to the survey.

A meal was an integral part of each session. During the first session, an overview description of the project was shared, and copies of the book, *Shift 2.0: Helping Congregations Back into the Game of Effective Ministry,* by Dr. Phil Maynard, were distributed. Everyone was asked to read a chapter of the book in preparation for the following week's group discussion. Participants were also asked to compile questions to ask during our upcoming church visits with congregational leaders so that the research team could learn best practices that could enhance CUMC's ministry.

Although not everyone attended each session, the process reached beyond the active participants and impacted and influenced those who participated in the research project as well as some key leaders who did not actively participate. One person who took the pre-test never attended any of the group sessions but read the book. That person also completed another book that leadership was asked to get to consider a capital campaign, entitled *Rich Church, Poor Church* by J. Cliff Christopher. That individual commented, after reading *Shift 2.0*, that CUMC has some growing to do. This insight from a leader not fully engaged in the process was helpful and provided hope. Another staff member/leadership team member attended two sessions and the final luncheon discussion which replaced the retreat.

Seven individuals attended the first session. Attrition by illness decreased the group by one more person. Two leaders participated sporadically due to travel schedules. One person, who took the survey, didn't join the group until later. Three additional individuals joined the group for Sunday, after church discussion sessions and church visits. On one Sunday, two, after-church, gatherings were scheduled - the Rooted Research Team and the Quarterly Planning Meeting. To accommodate both groups, which were comprised of members of the Leadership Council, the Quarterly Planning Meeting met first. Those present were invited to listen to the chapter conversation for Rooted and any insights from a church visit. Eleven individuals attended the closing retreat.

The following represents the actual project implementation schedule:

June 27, 2018 – Corresponded with Professional, Contextual and Peer Associates about the project timeline, surveys and proposed overview of implementation.

June 27, 2018 – Sent an email to the entire CUMC family through Realm sharing information about the research project.

July 3, 2018 – Shared a report about the upcoming Doctor of Ministry Project at the Leadership Council Meeting.

July 30, 2018 – Sent Implied Consent Letter for the Survey to the Leadership Members. A copy of the survey was included with the Consent Letter.

August 9, 2018 – Leadership Team received the electronic link to the survey.

August 31, 2018 – Another email invitation sent to Leadership Council members to take the survey.

September 7, 2018 – Corresponded with members of the Leadership Team, namely those who completed the electronic or paper survey to confirm the date and time of our group sessions.

Sunday, September 16, 2018 - First meeting with Research Team.

Sunday, September 23, 2018 11:30AM -12:30PM. Discuss Chapter 1 – "From Fellowship to Hospitality" (We will also identify which churches we will visit.)

Sunday, September 30, 2018 – Discuss Chapter 2 – "From Worship as an Event to Worship as a Lifestyle."

Sunday, October 7, 2018 – Discuss Chapter 3 "From Membership to Discipleship."

Wednesday, October 10, 2018 – Members of Rooted Research Team visited Cornerstone Assembly of God Church in Bowie, MD for dinner, worship and Bible studies.

Sunday, October 14, 2018 – Discuss Chapter 4 "From Serve Us to Service."

October 14, 2018 – Members of Rooted Research Team visited The Bridge, a New Faith Expression of Asbury United Methodist Church, Washington, D.C.

Sunday, October 21, 2018 – Discuss Chapter 5 "From Survival Mentality to Generosity" and participate in a Group Mission Experience.

Sunday, October 28, 2018 – Church Visit to First Baptist of Glenarden Church (In an attempt to engage the research team in one more church visit, the retreat was delayed a week.)

Sunday, November 4, 2018 – Closing 2-hour session at Fratelli's Italian Restaurant Meeting Room – Discussed insights from the process and identified takeaways that would benefit Cheverly United Methodist Church. We did not discuss the chapter, "Leading the Charge Without Getting Trampled." Our discussion did include next steps for implementation after the research project had ended. *The closing retreat was scheduled for Saturday, November 3, 2018 to be held at First UMC Hyattsville, MD. A family funeral pre-empted this plan and we adjusted to have the closing session on Sunday.

During each session, the group shared a meal, engaged scripture(s) related to the week's chapter focus and discussed the book or, when appropriate a church visit.

Highlights from Sunday, September 16, 2018

During the first session together, copies of the book, *Shift 2.0: Helping Congregations Back Into the Game of Effective Ministry,* were distributed and everyone was asked to read the first chapter and complete the chapter's questionnaire in preparation for the next session. As we contemplated which churches to visit, research project members suggested some criteria about which congregations to select. Some of those questions related to the criteria for selection included:

"Which congregations had success in increasing membership?"

"What are their best practices?"

"How can we become more financially strong?"

"How can we engage youth in ministry more effectively?"

"Can we include case studies from around the world?"

Interest was expressed about learning from congregations that were contextually similar. One such church was Tabor Presbyterian Church, in Portland, Oregon, a congregation that is centrally located in the community, and a place where numerous community organizations meet. Tabor Church successfully runs a coffee shop, something our congregation had previously considered.

It was understood that the church would need to reach beyond itself to connect with neighbors and discern the needs of the community. To address that need, neighbors would need to be asked," What do you need? The Child Parent Resource Center was suggested as a resource to engage community needs.

During the first session, participants not only learned more about the research project process, they were also invited to dream God dreams and imagine new possibilities. One person recommended breaking down some walls in the building to create a basketball court for the community teens to access. Other suggestions included creating a game room with pin ball machines, board games and computer games for community young people.

A list of proposed church visits was shared. Churches being considered for church visits either had gone through revitalization efforts or were multi-cultural faith communities. Congregations on the preliminary list were:

Cornerstone Church – A 2,000-member, multi-ethnic Assemblies of God congregation with 57 nations represented by persons worshipping there. According to the pastor, Rev. Mark Lehmann, when he arrived at the church, the conversations often centered around how to pay bills. The congregation has grown and desires to reach even more people for Christ.

First Baptist Church of Glenarden, an African American megachurch in Prince George's County that had gone through revitalization efforts under the leadership of the current pastor, Rev. John K Jenkins. A 2011 article recorded membership at 10,000. When Jenkins arrived, the congregation numbered 500 members.[199]

Emory Fellowship (United Methodist) – Located in Washington, DC, this congregation was slated for closure when the current pastor, the Rev. Joseph Daniels arrived 26 years ago. Together, the congregation and pastor have shared in a ministry that continues to transform the lives of neighbors. This multi-ethnic congregation numbers 650 people representing 24 nationalities, many of whom are from the African Diaspora.

Mt Oak Fellowship (United Methodist) – Located in Bowie, a community that boasts some of the same diversity present in Cheverly, this congregation has gone through revitalization. Currently the ministry provides ministries that reach and engage people beyond the church walls through Amped, "StreetReach,"and more. It is a Predominantly European American congregation that has a multi-ethnic and multi-cultural outreach.

Other congregations, one in College Park, MD and one in Alexandria, VA were suggested as an example to visit and learn from because of its game nights that encourage people to bring their own games. The churches that were ultimately selected for the visits were: Cornerstone Assemblies of God Church, The Bridge (Asbury United Methodist Church, DC) and

---

[199] First Baptist Church of Glenarden in the News, accessed December 9, 2018, https://www.washingtonpost.com/national/on-faith/where-we-worship-first-baptist-church-of-glenarden/2011/09/22/gIQAyi4HrK_story.html?noredirect=on&utm_term=.f4cb0704d406

First Baptist of Glenarden (MD). Asbury's Bridge Ministry was added to the list because of this African American Congregation's efforts to reach younger neighbors in a changing gentrifying community. Efforts were made to arrange conversations with church leadership during visits. Rooted Research Team participants were able to converse with leaders from Asbury UMC and Cornerstone Assemblies of God Church.

At the first gathering, everyone was asked to read chapter 1 of *Shift 2.0: Helping Congregations Back into the Game of Effective Ministry*. They were also asked to decide which church they would attend. Again, each person was asked to consider, from the readings and church visits practices and insights that could strengthen the ministry of CUMC.

Ethnically, the research team was very diverse. The original working group was comprised of eight individuals:

* Convener/Pastor – African American female
* An African American male youth (Youth Representative to Leadership Council)
* An African American female just over the young adult designation
* Two Anglo Females
* An Anglo Male
* An African American married heterosexual couple

The group met each Sunday, after worship, for one hour. Time together included discussion about a scripture related to a chapter of *Shift 2.0: Helping Congregations Back into the Game of Effective Ministry*, chapter insights and church visits. As time continued, three other individuals joined the group for study, discussion and church visits. They did not take the survey but participated with the group for learning.

The research team was scheduled to visit three churches – Cornerstone Assembly of God Church in Bowie, MD, Asbury United Methodist Church's *The Bridge*, Washington DC – A ministry targeting new, younger neighbors in the gentrifying neighborhood, and First Baptist Church of Glenarden. Rooted Research Team Members were able to meet with the pastoral leadership of Cornerstone and Asbury.

The research team created this list of questions to be used for conversations with church leadership were as follows:

1. Did you or do you now, have a program to increase church membership? If so, describe its plan.
2. How does your congregation recognize guests?
3. How does your congregation encourage regular participants to engage guests?
4. Do you have a plan to contact visitors' days/weeks after their visit?
5. Do you have a welcome packet for guests?
6. Do you have special programs for children, preteens, teens, young adults?
7. Do you have a certified nursery or day care?
8. What communication tools (website/social media/newsletter) do you find most beneficial?
9. What types of activities are provided to engage the community and to promote visibility?
10. What community services/outreach programs are you involved in?
11. What types of marketing tools are employed by this congregation?
12. Do your marketing efforts convey your church is open to all (race/sexual orientation/country of origin?)

The church visits were informative, engaging and a good way for CUMC leaders to learn from other congregations. Often, our knowledge is confined to our sphere of life. If the law of the lid is true for the pastor, it is also true for the lay leadership. The church visits enabled the congregational leaders to learn best practices from area churches. Each church visit provided insight into a distinct area of ministry. Cornerstone Church gave insight into hospitality, faith formation/disciple formation, worship, and multi-ethnic ministry. The Bridge (Asbury) shared how their congregation is actively trying to engage younger, Anglo-American neighbors as the downtown area gentrifies. The congregation also has numerous ministries to serve their homeless neighbors, including the Football Sunday meal and game in the Fellowship Hall, where the Bridge worships. First Baptist of Glenarden offered a glimpse into a congregation that emphasizes discipleship, community engagement and entrepreneurship, from a larger church perspective.

Church Visit Experiences and Insights

Cornerstone Assembly of God Church-Bowie, MD Wednesday Evening, Discipleship for All Ages, 7-8:30PM, Dinner served from 5:30-6:30PM. Church Visit: Wednesday, October 10, 2018

Although six members of the research team went to Cornerstone, only four were there in time to visit the Café to eat a meal before the short worship experience followed by the Bible study options. The Café provided chili, salad, bread and bottled water for a donation of $6.00 (Adults) and $4.00 (Children). Funds from the Café fund church missions. At the time of the visit, the Café had raised and donated more than $8,000 to missions. Bible study options included: children's, youth, men's, women's groups as well as a study on Romans.

Contact was made with Cornerstone Church's minister, Pastor Mark Lehmann through email and a personal contact through a church member. The church member's son and my son attend youth group together at First Baptist Church of Glenarden. Our team arrived separately, and each were greeted with warm hospitality. Numerous individuals even approached our youth team member, welcomed him to the church and invited him to the youth session. Pastor Mark had alerted staff to our visit. He also paid for our meal. Thinking we would return at another time to interview him or staff, he allowed us a short, impromptu interview in the Cafe before worship. The following recounts the exchange between Pastor Mark and those who shared a meal there.

1. Did or do you now, have a program to increase church membership? If so, describe its plan. "It is easier to increase membership than discipleship," Pastor Mark explained. "We need to raise the bar," he continued. He reported that each person who becomes a part of the Cornerstone Church family participates in a 7-week membership class and has expectations which include serving in ministry, regular worship attendance, giving through tithes and offerings, reaching out to the least and lost, inviting people to church, working for the unity of the church. Each person signs a membership covenant of expectations. "It is not about the

building," he stated. It is about being touched by God. It is not about the church and pastor.

Pastor Mark stressed the importance of discipleship. He added, "Discipleship is everyone's call. Membership is a choice." He added that churches need to raise the bar of expectation related to discipleship. Someone asked, "how do you get young people involved?" Pastor Mark replied, "get them connected with a passion for living and dying for God."

Pastor Mark continued, "this is the gospel- do you know what it means to trust God with the impossible?" He reiterated the importance of making disciples not members. "When you are waiting for God, don't make any compromises."

2. How does your congregation recognize guests? There is a Welcome Center for people to visit. There is a visitor reception each Sunday in a room near the Cornerstone Café.

3. How does your congregation encourage regular participants to engage guests? He explained, "It is part of the culture. It is in the covenant. It is what is taught in new member classes. Members of the congregation are trained to connect with visitors. It is part of the culture."

4. Do you have a plan to contact visitors' days/weeks after their visit? He calls every guest. Two other individuals call them. Guests will receive a letter also.

5. Do you have a welcome packet for guests? What is in it? Do you have a Welcome Center for guests? Cornerstone Church has a Welcome Center with information about the ministry opportunities.

6. Do you have special programs for children, preteens, teens, young adults? Yes.

7. Do you have a certified nursery or day care center? Yes

8. What communication tools (website/social media/newsletter) do you find most beneficial? No more mailers. Website and social media.

9. What types of activities are provided to engage the community and to promote visibility? 1/3 of their budget is given to mission. Additionally, through the Café, they have contributed $8,361.00 to missions. At Christmas, they give away gifts and coats. In the

fall they have a community outreach with petting zoo and more. All Free.

10. What community services/outreach programs are you involved in? At Christmas, they give away gifts and coats. In the fall they have a community outreach with petting zoo and more. All Free. They also support several missionaries.

11. What types of marketing tools are employed by this congregation? No more mailers. 1. Word of Mouth. 2)Facebook Ads 3) Wristbands with messages 4. Website

12. Do your marketing efforts convey your church is open to all (race/ sexual orientation/country of origin)? Our time ran out and we didn't have a chance to ask him this question as we needed to shift to go to worship before the discipleship classes.

The Bridge (Asbury UMC), Washington, DC
Sunday, 5:30PM, October 14, 2018

On Sunday,14, 2018, six members of the Rooted D. Min Project Team visited The Bridge, a ministry of Asbury UMC, 11th & K Streets, NW. To arrange a meeting, contact with the leadership of Asbury was made by email correspondence. Familiarity may have aided our connection. That church is the writer's home congregation.

Some of the group members had the opportunity to talk with Dr. Ianther Mills, Sr. Pastor of Asbury UMC, and Min. Matthew Wilke, Associate Pastor with responsibility for *The Bridge*. Min. Wilke explained to the group how he spent a year as Associate Pastor, preparing to launch the Bridge. They began by offering worship once a month and then weekly.

Dr. Ianther Mills began serving in ministry in 2013. Looking at the community's demographics from MissionInsite she realized that "this is not the DC that I grew up in." She explained that Asbury, a historic African American congregation, had to make a realization that the mission field had changed. We had "to embrace the new mission field." "Our mission is the same," she added, "the mission field has changed." "Asbury understands itself as a strong African American church, " Mills continued. "We still are...the church has to embrace the totality of its community."

In order to help Asbury embrace its changing community, a new strategy had to be created. Mills' strategy was to create a new, distinct, evening worship service, "not to upset the morning services." She explained "Blended worship doesn't make anyone happy." How can we truly blend the worship?" The Bridge strives to be multi-cultural, to have a blend of music – gospel, Hillsong, old hymns played in a contemporary fashion.

Asbury's church leadership understood, that in order to attract new neighbors, facility upgrades were necessary. To prepare their space to welcome the new neighbors, they renovated the fellowship hall. The project took $700,000 and includes an updated projection system, staging, sound system and more.

Dr. Mills and Min. Wilke responded to our questions before worship began. Here are the question responses.

1. Did or do you now, have a program to increase church membership? If so, describe its plan. Min. Matthew Wilke responded, "I'd much rather a plan for discipleship than membership." We have more of a plan to increase discipleship. We do it through small groups through the summer.

   Dr. Mills said, "Alpha (Bible Study) is foundational." "We have some small groups spin off from other small groups," she added. Asbury provides church-wide Bible studies in multiple locations - daytime, evening, in homes, even on-line through a conference call or skype Bible study.

   Due to limited time constraints before the worship service, the following related questions were asked together, at the same time.

2. How does your congregation recognize guests? 3. How does your congregation encourage regular participants to engage guests? 4. Do you have a plan to contact visitors to engage visitors days/weeks after their visit? 5. Do you have a welcome packet for guests...?

   Minister Wilke: "We ask everyone to fill out and turn in Connect Cards," and added "I personally call on Monday." He also sends a personal email. He often invites guests to meet somewhere for coffee, if they are open to it. Dr. Ianther Mills: "We give visitors a visitor folder and a letter is sent to them later."

3. Do you have special programs for children, preteens, teens, young adults?

   Min. Wilke: "We have Sunday School., VBS…not much of a youth group." "Small groups exist for young adults, most of whom are in their thirties."

4. Do you have a certified nursery or day care center? No.

5. What communication tools (website/social media/newsletter) do you find most beneficial? Constant Contact/Facebook/Instagram/Facebook Live.(They live stream through Facebook Live.) They have two websites – one for the Bridge and one for Asbury UMC. Min. Wilke shared his desire to use more video messages on social media. Google Ads are also a part of their strategy.

6. What types of activities are provided to engage the community and promote visibility? International Day (during Black History Month), Walk Throughs, First Fridays @ Asbury – a fusion of cultural, arts, dance, Jazz Vespers, and more.

7. What community service/outreach programs are you involved in? Food Pantry. Monthly Breakfast for and with homeless brothers and sisters – free medical care from Unity Health Care. Football Sundays consisting of a meal and showing of football games.

8. What types of marketing tools are employed by this congregation? They have two websites – one for the Bridge and one for Asbury UMC.

9. Do your marketing efforts convey your church is open to all (race/sexual orientation/country of origin)? International Sunday during Black History Month. Asbury is not a reconciling congregation.

First Baptist Church of Glenarden, Sunday, October 28, 2018 at 6:30PM

First Baptist Church of Glenarden is a predominantly African American congregation with various generations represented in worship. Only one person, this pastor, visited this church. Contact was made to arrange a meeting with church leadership through email. Efforts to meet with FBGC leadership didn't work out. Although no one else attended this church, some of the research team had worshipped there previously. Notes from the visit were taken and later shared with the rest of the Rooted

Research team. Those who had previously attended the church also shared their experience.

On each visit, the research team was asked to take in what they see and hear; how they are engaged by the church membership. The worship was held at the Worship Center in Upper Marlboro, MD. Hosting ministry in two locations, the congregation also has a Ministry Center in Landover, MD and an Empowerment Center in Landover, MD. Here were some observations from my visit.

Like the church I pastor, First Baptist Church of Glenarden began as a home study. Information on their website details how they had to transform from raising funds through fundraisers and special meals to God's way of tithing and proportional giving. The church also made the shift from membership to discipleship. Their mission and vision statement stress the congregation's discipleship emphasis. "The First Baptist Church of Glenarden has been called and appointed by God to serve this community for His glory. We purpose and are committed to fulfilling our mandate and vision. "Developing Dynamic Disciples through Discipleship, Discipline and Duplication."

Although not able to meet with church leadership, many of the answers to the groups' questions were available from the church website. The responses to the group questions are made by observation and checking the website. It was not as planned in the project but did provide information.

1. Did you or do you now, have a program to increase church membership? Is so, describe its plan. According to the website, the church offers biblical teaching each day of the week.[200] Alpha Bible study and other courses are offered.

2. How does your congregation recognize guests? Guests were recognized by completing a contact form and turning it into the welcome center near the front entrance. I didn't turn in a form and can't report on the follow up from the church.

3. How does your congregation encourage regular participants to engage guests? Is it part of the culture? In the service, the pastoral

---

[200] First Baptist Church of Glenarden Website "I Am New," accessed December 15, 2018, http://www.fbcglenarden.org/i-am-new/classes.html.

leadership invited each person to greet and meet the person(s) beside them and then pray with them, holding hands.

4. Do you have a plan to contact visitors' days/weeks after their visit? Don't have that answer because I was unable to ask and didn't turn in a member card.

5. Do you have a welcome packet for guests? A gift of some kind is given to guests at the Welcome Center.

6. Do you have special programs for children, preteens, teens, young adults, etc.? Yes. The church offers Cub & Boy Scouts and an extensive list of ministries for young people of all ages.

7. Do you have a certified nursery or day care center? FBCG's Shabach Ministries, Inc. offers day care and elementary school kindergarten through 6th grade, and a K-12 home school administration program.

8. What communication tools (website/social media/newsletter) do you find most beneficial? Not sure but the church uses Facebook, twitter and YouTube. FBCG also broadcasts worship services on a DC Radio One station. Worship and Prayer Services are live streamed and archived. The church also has a Mobile App and "on-demand tv."

9. What types of activities are provided to engage the community and to promote visibility? Free concerts, health fairs, college fairs, and holiday programs featuring well known musical artists are just a few things they offer the community. The church just opened its Family Life Building. The facility, built debt free, offers a work out room open to the community.

10. What community services/outreach programs are you involved in? Spiritual counseling, food distribution and Spanish Translation and Sign Language for worship.

11. What types of marketing tools are employed by this congregation? Radio ads are on area radio stations. Website. Not sure what else.

12. Do your marketing efforts convey your church is open to all (race/sexual orientation/country of origin? Didn't have the opportunity to ask the question. The church does offer classes, "All Things New: Healing for Unwanted Same Sex Attraction."

Summary of Learning

Qualitative research strives to understand the foundational underpinnings of a situation or problem related to the thoughts, opinions, insights and motives of individuals.[201] This research project sought to prove my hypothesis. My hypothesis was that disciple making in the congregation had diminished, which was caused by and the result of a loss of understanding of the mission of the church and a low prioritization of reaching new people for Christ, even the hundreds of people God brings into the church building weekly. The research supported my hypothesis in multiple ways. The elements that I cite for support of the hypothesis are: group discussions about church visits/book, the book questionnaires, follow up plans created and implemented by various ministries, and responses to additional questions posed to gain additional understanding. As a result of the research project, demonstrated qualitative responses were evident in the actions of the research project participants.

The closing retreat, held over a meal at a community restaurant, revealed new ways of approaching ministry by people around the table. Those present agreed that there are several things that the leaders and congregation need to and can do to strengthen the ministry. The take-aways from the afternoon, all related to congregational revitalization and strengthening discipleship were:

- The financial information and testimonies would make a difference.
- The new approach for greeters who introduce themselves to guests is a big step. The congregation needs to know what to do to greet guests. Everyone is invited to meet those around them. It will help cultivate a culture of hospitality.
- The Mission and Vision Statement should be on the bulletin again.
- We need to tie our giving to the mission. The Social Creed is one way to connect our mission and giving.

---

[201] Susan E. DeFranco, SnapSurveys, September 16, 2011. Accessed on December 13, 2018, https://www.snapsurveys.com/blog/qualitative-vs-quantitative-research/.

- Provide a daily, on-line devotional to members. Possibly create a sermon series and offer a related devotional for members.
- Enlist a mystery worship visitor to find out how we are perceived and welcome guests
- Develop a mentor program for new members
- Create small groups
- Meet in an on-going way to continue strengthening CUMC's ministry
- Create a narrative budget
- Tithe the church's budget
- Strengthen the greeting/usher ministry

At the retreat, various people confirmed that the shift from membership to discipleship is important. One participant shared that, only two other ministries he participated in stressed the importance of discipleship – a monastic community in the northeast and one in Sri Lanka. He stressed the need to encourage others to grow as disciples. He said, "We can invite people in the prayer times on Tuesdays. 'If people saw themselves as disciples and all that it means...how do we help people come to understand this? How do we help people understand who they are in Christ?'"

The pre-research and post-research surveys were helpful in providing information about how research project team participants believed and acted prior to and after the project. The pre-research and post-research were not helpful in gauging major shifts in thinking. Only minor changes were indicated or detected by the pre and post research surveys. One individual reported a change in perspective about inviting people to attend worship. When the project started, the individual reported not inviting people to worship because "I'm embarrassed and/or afraid to invite someone to church. At the end of the research project, the person reported that the individual still does not invite people to attend worship because "Religion is a private issue. I don't want to impose my beliefs on anyone else." While not ready to invite people to worship, the person did shift related to inviting people to other non-worship activities in the church. At the beginning of the research project the person reported not inviting people to church activities. By the end of the project, the individual reported inviting people to other church activities: picnics, programs, etc.

Survey Highlights and Insights

Final Insights

For the most part, the project went well. In hindsight, I wouldn't have scheduled a mission project and may not have initially planned a half day retreat. Scheduling group sessions was a challenge and for the short amount of time allocated for the project, it was an adventure of coordination. Another approach to communicate the research project emphasis may have encouraged more participation by other leaders. It may have been better to share how the project would identify ways to further strengthen the ministry of the church, although I'm not sure anything would have encouraged more people to take part in the project. Some interest grew after people heard about what the research project team was doing.

The church visits were an asset to the process. It would have been nice to visit other churches to learn best practices. Although no one visited First Baptist Church of Glenarden, I plan to invite church leaders to attend another worship service, concert or activity there. It is my belief that it is important to learn from and know about ministries of larger congregations in the community that are especially known to people in the area.

The adage, "Rome wasn't built in a day" is true. Just as the church's current situation didn't happen overnight, neither will the revitalization. Congregational transformation and revitalization are a process that take time. At the completion of the research project much work still needs to be done. Going forward, continued emphasis on discipleship, is a must. Members of the research project, and others who want to share in this effort will be called back together to learn about discipleship and reaching the community with God's love. It will be important to create an intentional discipleship system that provides opportunities for disciples at different places on the journey, to be and grow. One size does not fit all.

Resources that may be useful, in small group settings like the research project, and church wide sermon series, include:

Developing An Intentional Discipleship System: A Guide for Congregations by Junius B. Dotson

Engaging Your Community: A Guide to Seeing All the People
by Junius B. Dotson

Membership to Discipleship by Phil Maynard

The church's discipleship opportunities will need to stress the importance of duplication. Discipleship has a direct correlation with duplication as people are oriented to their roles and calling. When Christ followers understand their mission and calling, their thoughts and actions usually change.

To really influence the ministry of the church, discipleship and duplication and evangelism will need to become integrated into all areas of ministry so that the culture of the congregation can change. That emphasis will need to be included for everyone, from the youngest to the most seasoned saint. New Members' Classes will need to be designed to help people engage who they are as disciples and encourage them to live that out in their homes, on their jobs, and in their communities. All of this will help the congregation be externally focused toward those who are not part of the church family- neighbors or those who come into the church building for various meetings and purposes. Disciple making will need to become a major priority in the life of the congregation so that it can fulfill its mission and God assignment in the community. It is through this continued effort that Cheverly United Methodist Church can not only be the "church in the heart of the community with the community in its heart," but the church that shows and shares God's heart with the people of Cheverly, 20785 and beyond. May it be so!

APPENDIX

SMALL GROUP PARTICIPANTS WERE ASKED to complete a pre-research and post-research survey to gauge any difference or growth. The questions for both surveys are as follows:

1. Do you engage in personal devotions during the week?
2. What do you use in your personal devotion?
3. How often do you read the bible or a devotional?
4. How often do you attend worship?
5. Do you invite people to attend worship service?
6. Why or why not?
7. As a practice, do you invite people to other church activities: picnics, programs, etc?
8. Why or why not?
9. What is the mission of the church?
10. Do you participate in any of the faith formation opportunities at church: Bible study, Sunday School or Small group?
11. If not, why?
12. Is faith-sharing a role or responsibility of a Christian?
13. Do you share your faith?
14. If not, why?

BIBLIOGRAPHY

Achtemeier, Paul. *Harper's Bible Dictionary*. San Francisco, CA: Harper Collins, 1985.

Agnes, Michael, editor. *Webster's New World Compact Desk Dictionary*. Cleveland, OH: Wiley Publishing, Inc. 2002, 499-500.

Andrews, Dale P. and Robert London Smith, Jr., editors. *Black Practical Theology*. Waco, TX: Baylor University Press, 2015.

Atkins, Derek. "Reimagining Faith Formation." February 7, 2014. Accessed December 20, 2017. https://thebanner.org/features/2014/02/reimagining-faith-formation, 2014.

Awabdy, Mark A. "YHWH Exegetes Torah, How Ezekiel 44: 7-9 Bars Foreigners from the Sanctuary." *Journal of Biblical Literature*, (January 1, 2012): 685-703. Accessed March 16, 2017. https://www.academia.edu/3500134/YHWH_Exegetes_Torah_How_Ezek_44_7-9_Bars_Foreigners_from_the_Sanctuary.

Beegle, Dewey M. *Prophecy and Prediction*. Ann Arbor, MI: Pryor Pettengill, 1978.

Book of Discipline. Paragraph 252 "What We Believe." Accessed November 23, 2018. http://www.umc.org/what-we-believe/para-252-the-church-council.

Bosch, David J. *Transforming Mission: Paradigm Shifts in Theology of Mission*.

Maryknoll, NY: Orbis Books, 1991.

———. *Witness to the World: The Christian Mission in Theological Perspective*.

Atlanta, GA: John Knox Press, 1980.

Brim, Billye. "How to Use Your God-Given Authority." Sid Roth's *It's Supernatural*. YouTube Video. Accessed February 13, 2018. https://www.youtube.com/watch?v=c-HH1VhzMXI.

Brown, Olu. Impact Lead Team with Christine Shinn Latona. *Zero to 80: Innovative Ideas for Planting and Accelerating Church Growth*. Atlanta, GA: Impact Press. 2010.

Bruggemann, Walter. *The Prophetic Imagination*. Philadelphia, PA: Fortress Press, 1978.

Bush, Joseph Jr. *Practical Theology in Church and Society*. Eugene, OR: Cascade Books, 2016.

Buttrick, George Arthur, John Knox, Herbert Gordon May. *The Interpreter's Dictionary of the Bible: An Illustrated Encyclopedia, R-Z, Volume 4*. Nashville: Abingdon Press, 1989.

Coates, Ta-Nehisi, *Between the World and Me*. Accessed December 5, 2016. https://www.goodreads.com/author/quotes/1214964.Ta_Nehisi_Coates.

Cordle, Steve. *The CHURCH in Many HOUSES: Reaching Your Community Through Cell-Based Ministry*. Nashville, TN: Abingdon Press, 2005.

DeFranco, Susan E. "SnapSurveys." September 16, 2011. Accessed December 13, 2018. https://www.snapsurveys.com/blog/qualitative-vs-quantitative-research/.

de Hoop, Raymond. "The Interpretation of Isaiah 56: 1-9, Comfort or Criticism?," *Journal of Biblical Literature*, 127, no 4, (Winter 2008): 671-695. Accessed March 28, 2017. http://web.a.ebscohost.com.utsdayton.idm.oclc.org/ehost/pdfviewer/pdfviewer?vid=12&sid=566d7b02-cb1f-4f22-845a-39589eaeeb6e%40sessionmgr4007.

Engelsviken, Tormod. "Spiritual Conflict: A Challenge for the Church in the West with a View to the Future." *Paradigm Shifts in Christian Witness: Insights from Anthropology, Communication and Spiritual Power*. Maryknoll, NY: Orbis Books, 2008.

Engle, Lou. "AzusaNow! The 110th Anniversary of the Azusa Street Revival." *BreakingChristian News*, Pasadena, CA. Published by *Breaking Christian News*, Mar 1, 2016 by *The Elijah List*. Accessed May 5, 2017. http://www.breakingchristiannews.com/articles/display_art.html?ID=17699.

Enns, Peter. "Isaiah." 2011-2017. Accessed March 31, 2017. http://thecenterforbiblicalstudies.org/resources/introductions-to-the-books-of-the-bible/isaiah/.

Erdkamp, Paul. "Jews and Christians at the dinner table: a study in social and religious

Interaction." Accessed March 28, 2017. http://www.academia.edu/4752200/Jews_and_Christians_at_the_dinner_table._A_study_in_social_and_religious_interaction.

Farr, Bob with Kay Kotan. *Renovate or Die. Ten Ways to Focus Your Church on Mission*. Nashville, TN: Abingdon Press, 2011.

"Feast of Pentecost." Accessed February 19, 2018. https://www.thoughtco.com/feast-of-pentecost-700186.

"First Baptist Church in the News." Accessed December 9, 2018. https://www.washingtonpost.com/national/on-faith/where-we-worship-first-baptist-church-of-glenarden/2011/09/22/gIQAyi4HrK_story.html?noredirect=on&utm_term=.f4cb0704d406.

"First Fifty Years: 1942-1992." Cheverly United Methodist Church. Cheverly, Maryland.

5 things to know about Om."Hindu American, accessed May 31, 2022. https://www.hinduamerican.org/blog/5-things-to-know-about-om#:~:text=The%20word%20Om%20is%20defined,vibrations%20are%20able%20to%20manifest.

Flanders, Henry Jackson, Jr., Robert Wilson Crapps and David Anthony Smith. *An Introduction to the Old Testament: People of the Covenant, Third Edition*. New York, NY: Oxford University Press, 1988.

General Council on Finance and Administration. "Membership by Ethnicity," United Methodist Data. Demographic Information for Cheverly United Methodist Church Compiled by Whitney Washington, Research Office Coordinator. Accessed September 27, 2016. https://mail.google.com/mail/u/0/#label/church+demographics/156e6c43f9b3a7b8?projec tor=1.

Gertz, Stephen. "What is the pre-Christian history of the baptismal ceremony?" *Christianity Today*. Posted August 8, 2008. Accessed April 13, 2017. http://www.christianitytoday.com/history/2008/august/what-is-pre-christian-history-of-baptismal-ceremony.html.

Glover, Dan and Claudia Lavy. *Deepening Your Effectiveness: Restructuring the Local Church for Life Transformation*. Nashville, TN: Discipleship Resources, 2006.

Goldingay, J. *Isaiah 56-66 (International Critical Commentary): A Critical and Exegetical Commentary*. London, UK: Bloomsbury Publishing, 2014. Accessed February 5, 2018. http://dx.doi.org/10.5040/9781472556158.0008.

Grady, J. Lee. "Pentecostals Renounce Racism," December 12, 1994. Accessed May 19, 2017. http://www.christianitytoday.com/ct/1994/december12/4te058.html.

"Guidelines: The UMC and the Charismatic Movement," approved by 1976 General Conference. Accessed May 24, 2017. http://www.umc.org/what-we-believe/guidelines-the-umc-and-the-charismatic-movement.

Hall, Marlon. "Faith and Innovation," (a lecture delivered at the Immerse Conference: Where Spirituality and Innovation Connect," St. John's Downtown UMC, Houston, TX). March 17, 2017.

Halloran, Kevin. "Christian Doctor's Digest." Featuring Richard Foster on the Celebration of Discipline: The Path to Spiritual Growth, Part 1. YouTube video. Accessed October 17, 2017. Posted (February 19, 2013). https://www.youtube.com/watch?v=9BJmAJjh-OY.

———. "Christian Doctor's Digest." Featuring Richard Foster on the Celebration of Discipline: The Path to Spiritual Growth, Part 2. Youtube video. Posted (February 19, 2013). Accessed October 17, 2017. https://www.youtube.com/watch?v=Kw3Tgow1V3A.

Hannah-Jones, Nicole. "Almost 50 Years After MLK, Why Is the Church So Racially Divided?" Interview by Morgan Lee. *Christian Post.* Published (January 28, 2014) YouTube video. Accessed May 10, 2017. https://www.youtube.com/watch?v=SpheIwG2GWM.

Harris, Laura Henry. "Coffey Chapel's Revitalization." Email, September 8, 2016. Spiritual Autobiography.

———. "Overcoming the Deaf and Dumb Spirit." Video. Accessed September 9, 2017. http://www.whereheleadsme.org/teaching-videos.html.

Hayes, Christopher B. "The Book of Isaiah in Contemporary Research." *Religion Compass.* Hoboken, NJ: Blackwell Publishing, 2011: 558. Accessed March 31, 2017. http://www.academia.edu/1883357/The_Book_of_Isaiah_in_ Contemporary_Research.

"History Matters: The US Survey Course on the Web." Accessed May 10, 2017. http://historymatters.gmu.edu/d/5478/.

Hirsch, Alan and Debra Hirsch. *Untamed: Reactivating a Missional Form of Discipleship.* Grand Rapids, MI: Baker Books, 2010.

Hjalmeby, Erik J. "A Rhetorical History of Race Relations in the Early Pentecostal Movement, 1906-1916." M.A. thesis, Baylor University, Waco, TX, 2007. Accessed December 27, 2017. https://baylor-ir.tdl.org/baylor-ir/bitstream/handle/2104/5062/erik_hjalmeby_masters.pdf?sequence=1.

Holladay, Carl R. "Acts." *Harper's Bible Commentary.* San Francisco, CA: Harper SanFrancisco, 1988.

"How Holy Roller Gets Religion." California Digital Newspaper Collection, *Los Angeles*

Herald, no. 33, no. 345 (September 10, 1906). Accessed May 20, 2017. https://cdnc.ucr.edu/cgi-bin/cdnc?a=d&d=LAH19060910.2.94.

"I Am New." First Baptist Church of Glenarden website. Accessed December 15, 2018. http://www.fbcglenarden.org/i-am-new/classes.html.

Johnson, Alan R. "An Anthropological Approach to the Study of Leadership: Lessons learned on Improving Leadership Practice." *Transformation 24/3* (July & October 2007): 213-221. Accessed December 12, 2017. http://thaimissions.info/gsdl/collect/thaimiss/index/assoc/HASH468a.dir/doc.pdf.

Johnson, Keith L. *Theology as Discipleship*. Downers Grove, IL: InterVarsity Press, 2015.

Jordan, Miriam, "Trump Administration Ends Temporary Protection for Haitians." *New York Times*, November 20, 2017. Accessed November 23, 2017. https://www.nytimes.com/2017/11/20/us/haitians-temporary-status.html.

Joyner, Rick. *The Power to Change the World: The Welsh and Azusa Street Revivals*. Fort Mill, SC: MorningStar Publications, Inc., 2010. Accessed November 24, 2017. http://eaglemissions.org/wp-content/uploads/2012/04/powertoChangeWorld.pdf.

King, J. D. "Why the Azusa Street Revival Ended." *Charisma News*, April 16, 2016. Accessed May 5, 2017. http://www.charismanews.com/opinion/56476-why-the-azusa-street-revival-ended.

King, Jr., Martin Luther. Interview on *Meet the Press*. April 17, 1960. YouTube video. Accessed May 10, 2017. https://www.youtube.com/watch?v=1q881g1L_d8.

————.. "Letter from a Birmingham Jail." Accessed February 26, 2018. https://www.africa.upenn.edu/Articles_Gen/Letter_Birmingham.html.

Kinnamon, David. "2015 State of Atheism." *Articles in Faith & Christianity*, March 24, 2015. Accessed March 31, 2017. https://www.barna.com/research/2015-state-of-atheism-in-america/.

————. "New Research on the State of Discipleship." *Research Releases in Leaders & Pastors*, December 1, 2015. Accessed April 2, 2017. https://www.barna.com/research/new-research-on-the-state-of-discipleship/.

Klein, Ralph W. *Israel in Exile: A Theological Interpretation*. Philadelphia, PA: Fortress Press, 1979.

Knight, Henry H., III. *From Aldersgate to Azusa Street: Wesleyan, Holiness, and Pentecostal Visions of the New Creation*. Eugene, OR: Pickwick Publications, 2010.

Leadership Resources, "The 15 Best James Hudson Taylor Quotes." Accessed December 14, 2016. http://www.leadershipresources.org/the-15-best-james-hudson-taylor-quotes/.

Levine, Amy-Jill and Marianne Blickenstaff, ed. *A Feminist Companion to the Acts of the Apostles*. New York, NY: T&T Clark International, 2004.

Levine, Amy-Jill and Marc Zvi Brettler, *The Jewish Annotated New Testament: New Revised Standard Version Bible Translation*. New York, NY: Oxford University Press, Inc., 2011.

Liardon, Roberts. "God's Generals: William J. Seymour," (video). Accessed May 27, 2017. http://godsgenerals.com/williamseymour/.

Library of Congress. "America at the Turn of the Century: A Look at the Historical Context." Accessed May 9, 2017. https://www.loc.gov/collections/early-films-of-new-york-1898-to-1906/articles-and-essays/america-at-the-turn-of-the-century-a-look-at-the-historical-context/.

Lipka, Michael. "A Closer Look at America's Rapidly Growing Religious Nones," Pew Research Center. Accessed March 31, 2017. http://www.pewresearch.org/fact-tank/2015/05/13/a-closer-look-at-americas-rapidly-growing-religious-nones/.

Long, Brad. Video and script for "Discerning Strongholds in the Local Church-Introduction," Recorded February 13, 2014. Accessed December 8, 2017. http://discernwith.us/discerning-strongholds-in-the-local-church-introduction.

"Los Angeles: The Apostolic Faith Mission." *The Apostolic Faith, Volume 1, No 2.* October 1906. Accessed May 20, 2017. http://pentecostalarchives.org/digitalPublications/USA/Independent/Apostolic%20Faith%20(Azusa%20Street)/Unregistered/1906/FPHC/1906_10.pdf#search="Apostolic Faith".

Martin, Larry. *The Life and Ministry of William J. Seymour and a History of the Azusa Street Revival.* Joplin, MO: Christian Life Books, 1999.

Maupin, Gary. "Spiritual Housecleaning" (Videos, Part 1, 2, 3 & 4). Accessed December 13, 2017. http://www.whereheleadsme.org/teaching-videos.html.

Maynard, Phil. *Shift 2.0: Helping Congregations Back into the Game of Effective Ministry.* Knoxville, TN: Market Square Publishing Company, LLC, 2018.

McGee, Gary B. "William J. Seymour and the Azusa Street Revival," *Enrichment Journal*, Springfield, MO: The General Council of the Assemblies of God, 2017. Accessed May 20, 2017. http://enrichmentjournal.ag.org/199904/026_azusa.cfm.

Menzie, Nicola. "Martin Luther King Jr.'s I Have A Dream Speech Turns 50; Surprising Facts About MLK's Historic Remarks." Accessed December 6, 2016. http://www.christianpost.com/news/martin-luther-king-jrs-i-have-a-dream-speech-turns-50-surprising-facts-about-mlks-historic-remarks-103144/.

Miller, David. "Missiology." Accessed October 13, 2017. https://www.theologynetwork.org/theology-of-everything/missiology.htm.

MissionInsite, Quadrennium Report, MissionInsite, Quadrennium Project, American Beliefs, Preferences & Practices, Date of Report, October 25, 2016.

Moore, Art. "Church Growth: Spiritual Mapping Gains Credibility Among Leaders,"

Christianity Today, Posted January 12, 1998. Accessed December 13, 2017. http://www.christianitytoday.com/ct/1998/january12/8t1055.html.

Napier, B. Davie. "From Faith to Faith—Essays on Old Testament Literature." Accessed February 12, 2018. http://www.religion-online.org/book-chapter/chapter-5-law-i-hear-0-israel-the-legal-codesi/.

Neff, David. "Biblical Adoption is Not What You Think it Is." November 22, 2013. Accessed March 16, 2017. http://www.christianitytoday.com/ct/2013/december/heirs-biblicaliblical-take-on-adoption.html.

Neil, William. *The Acts of the Apostles*. London, UK: Oliphants-Marshall, Morgan & Scott, 1973.

Newbigin, Lesslie. *The Open Secret: An Introduction to the Theology of Mission*. Grand Rapids, MI: Wm. B. Eerdmans Publishing Co., 1995.

Newsome, Carol A. and Sharon H. Ringe. *The Women's Bible Commentary*. Louisville, KY: Westminster/John Knox Press, 1992.

Nguyen, Van Thanh, SVD. "Dismantling Cultural Boundaries: Missiological Implications of Acts 10:1-11:18," *Missiology An International Review*, Vol XL, no. 4, (October 2012). Accessed December 5, 2017. http://web.a.ebscohost.com.utsdayton.idm.oclc.org/ehost/pdfviewer/pdfviewer?vid=1&sid=1afedd51-fd1e-47b5-802c-a63447cb0942%40sessionmgr4006.

Niche. "Best Suburbs to live in Washington, D.C. Metro," *The Niche* 2016 List of Best Places to Live. Accessed November 11, 2016. https://local.niche.com/rankings/suburbs/best-suburbs/m/washington-dc-metro-area/.

Nixon, Paul. *Healing Spiritual Amnesia: Remembering What It Means to Be the Church*.

Nashville: Abington Press, 2004.

Ogden, Greg. "The Discipleship Deficit: Where Have All the Disciples Gone?" *Knowing & Doing*. C.S. Lewis Institute, 2011. Accessed April 2, 2017. http://www.cslewisinstitute.org/The_Discipleship_Deficit_SinglePage.

Osborne, Larry. *Sticky Church*. Grand Rapids, MI: Zondervan, 2008.

Owens, Robert R. *Speak to the Rock: The Azusa Street Revival*. Lanham, MD: University Press of America. 1998.

Parker, Julie Faith. "Children in the Hebrew Bible, Bible Odyssey." Accessed March 16, 2017. https://www.bibleodyssey.org/en/passages/related-articles/children-in-the-hebrew-bible.

"Philippine-American War, 1899–1902." Office of the Historian. Accessed May 10, 2017. https://history.state.gov/milestones/1899-1913/war.

Rackham, Richard Belward. *The Acts of the Apostles: An Exposition*. London, UK: Methuen & Co. Ltd., 1939.

Readiness 360: Multiply Your Impact. Readiness 360 Complete Report. Readiness 360, LLC, 2016.

Reddie, Anthony G. *Is God Colour-Blind? Insights from Black Theology for Christian Ministry*. London: Society for Promoting Christian Knowledge, 2009.

Robeck Jr., Cecil M. *The Azusa Street Mission and Revival: The Birth of the Global Pentecostal Movement*. Nashville, TN: Thomas Nelson Publishers, 2006.

———. "THE PAST: Historical Roots of Racial Unity and Division in American Pentecostalism." Accessed May 20, 2017. http://www.pctii.org/cyberj/cyberj14/robeck.pdf.

Russell, Rusty. "Temple Warning Inscription, Bible History Online." Accessed November 24, 2017. http://www.bible-history.com/archaeology/israel/temple-warning.html.

Seymour, William J. "The Precious Atonement." William Seymour articles and sermons. Accessed May 17, 2017. http://www.serhmonindex.net/modules/articles/index.php?view=category&cid=329.

———. *The Words that Changed the World: Azusa Street Sermons*. Joplin, MO: Christian Life Books, 1999.

Smetlana, Bob. "Sunday Morning in America is Still Segregated-And That's Ok With Worshipers." LifeWay Research, 2014. Posted January 15, 2015. Accessed May 11, 2017. http://lifewayresearch. com/2015/01/15/sunday-morning-in-america-still-segregated-and-thats-ok-with-worshipers/.

Smith, Eddie and Alice Smith. *Spiritual Housecleaning: Protect Your Home and Family From Spiritual Pollution.* Bloomington, MN: Chosen Books, 2015.

Smith, Paul Allen. *Rhetoric and Redaction in Trito-Isaiah, The Structure, Growth and Authorship of Isaiah 56-66.* Philadelphia, PA: Fortress Press 1971.

"Sparking A Discipleship Movement in America and Beyond." CS Lewis Institute, 2011. Accessed April 2, 2017. http://www.cslewisinstitute. org/webfm_send/210.

Stetzer, Ed. "What is a Missiologist? The Theology, Tools, and a Team of a Missiologist. *Christianity Today* (June 10, 2013). Accessed November 26, 2017. https://www.christianitytoday.com/ edstetzer/2013/june/what-is-missiologist.html.

Strong's Concordance. Glossa, γλῶσσα, 1100. Accessed March 30, 2017. http://biblehub.com/greek/1100.htm.

Strong's Concordance. "6666. Tsedaqah." Accessed March 23, 2017. http:// biblehub.com/hebrew/6666.htm.

Strong's Concordance. "3444. yeshuah: salvation." Accessed March 23, 2017. http://biblehub.com/hebrew/3444.htm.

Synan, Vinson. "Interview with Lawrence Katly and Mattie Cummings." (June 17, 2014.) Youtube Video. Accessed May 29, 2017. https:// www.youtube.com/watch?v=THOCgQqWKFo.

———. "Pentecostalism: William Seymour, Issue 65: Ten Influential Christians of the 20ˢᵗ Century." Christianity Today.com. Accessed May 9, 2017. http://www.christianitytoday.com/history/issues/ issue65/pentecostalism-william-seymour.html.

312 Azusa.com. Accessed May 20, 2017.

Tiffany, Frederick C. and Sharon Ringe. *Biblical Interpretation: A Road Map*. Nashville, TN: Abingdon Press, 1996.

2016 Sperling's Best Places. Accessed December 12, 2016. http://www.bestplaces.net/city/maryland/cheverly.

United Methodist Mission Statement. Accessed December 28, 2017. http://www.umc.org/news-and-media/united-methodist-mission-statement-revised.

USA City Facts. "Cheverly Population by Age." Accessed December 13, 2017. http://www.usacityfacts.com/md/prince-george-s/cheverly/population/.

Van Engen, Charles E., Darrell Whiteman, & J. Dudley Woodberry, editors. *Paradigm Shifts in Christian Witness: Insights from Anthropology, Communication, and Spiritual Power*. Maryknoll, NY: Orbis, 2008.

"Walking Tour of Cheverly." Accessed November 10, 2016. https://drive.google.com/file/d/0BwFvqsBgQJK1ZjQ2OTk3YTctNGM3NS0 0ZTkzLWJmMmMtNWU0NjBkZjk2NzVl/view.

Ware, Gabrielle. "UN Warns US to Fight Racism After Charlottesville." (August 24, 2017.) Accessed November 23, 2017. https://www.newsy.com/stories/un-is-alarmed-by-racist-events-in-us-gives-stern-warning/.

Wesley Center for Applied Theology. "The Scripture Way of Salvation." Wesley Center Online. Northwest Nazarene University, 1999. Accessed May 24, 2017. http://wesley.nnu.edu/john-wesley/the-sermons-of-john-wesley-1872-edition/sermon-43-the-scripture-way-of-salvation/.

Wesley, John. *The Holy Spirit & Power*. Edited by Clare Weakley. Alachua, FL: Bridge-Logos, 2003.

————. "Thoughts Upon Methodism." London: August 4, 1786. Accessed December 12, 2016.file:///C:/Users/pastor/Downloads/THOUGHTS_UPON_METHODISM.PDF.

Whiteman, Darrell L. "One Significant Solution: How Anthropology Became the Number One Study For Evangelical Missionaries. Part 1: Anthropology and Mission: The Incarnational Connection." *International Journal of Frontier Missions.* (Winter 2003.) Accessed December 12, 2017. http://www.ijfm.org/PDFs_IJFM/21_1_PDFs/35_44_Whiteman2.pdf.

Williams, Jeffrey. *Religion and Violence in Early American Methodism: Taking the Kingdom by Force.* Bloomington, IN: Indiana University Press, 2010.

"World's Largest Single Church with 800,000 members." Accessed December 13, 2017. https://www.youtube.com/watch?v=25Jpdfip8-4.

Wright, Jacob L. and Michael J. Chan. "King and Eunuch: Isaiah 56:1-8 in Light of Honorific Royal Burial Practices," *Journal of Biblical Literature,* 131, no. 1 (2012): 99-119. Accessed March 28, 2017. http://web.a.ebscohost.com.utsdayton.idm.oclc.org/ehost/detail/detail?vid=7&sid=566d7b02-cb1f-4f22-845a-39589eaeeb6e%40sessionmgr4007&bdata=JnNpdGU9ZWhvc3QtbGl2ZQ%3d%3d#AN=ATLA0001886158&db=rfh. Zaqantov, Yochanan. "The Ger, Gur, Zur, Nekar, Nakar, Goy and Lavah." Accessed February 12, 2018. http://www.karaitejudaism